What's up with my DOG?

What's up with my DOG?

Dr. Bruce Fogle

DK Dorling Kindersley
LONDON, NEW YORK, MUNICH,
MELBOURNE, DELHI

First published in the United States 2002
by DK Publishing, Inc., 95 Madison Avenue,
New York, NY 10016

2 4 6 8 10 9 7 5 3 1

Library of Congress Cataloging-in-Publication
Data

Fogle, Bruce
   What's up with my dog? / Bruce Fogle.--
1st American ed.
      p. cm.
ISBN 0-7894-8406-4 (alk. paper)
1. Dogs--Diseases. 2. Dogs--Health. I. Title.

SF991 .F5743 2002
636.7'0896--dc21
                          2001047625

What's Up With My Dog? provides general
information on a wide range of animal health
and veterinary topics. The book is not a
substitute for advice from a qualified veterinary
practitioner. You are advised always to consult
your veterinary surgeon or other appropriate
expert if you have specific queries in relation
to your pet's health. The naming of any
organisation or product in this book does not
imply endorsement by the publisher and the
omission of any such names does not indicate
disapproval. The publisher and author are not
responsible for any loss, injury, or damage
allegedly arising from any information or
suggestion in this book.

Color reproduced by Bright Arts, Singapore.
Printed and bound in Slovakia by TBB.

See our complete product line at
www.dk.com

CONTENTS

PART TWO
SYMPTOMS CHARTS

INTRODUCTION

It took me a little while to realize that one of the reasons that the dog is our best friend is because the two of us are so much alike. Both of us are gregariously sociable species, and we share an everlasting curiosity about life. We both enjoy play as an end in itself, rather than as a learning process. We both remain forever kids at heart.

This is enormously helpful when determining what's happening to your dog. The dog has a sophisticated array of body language signals that are as good as ours – better in fact. Can you use your ears and tail to let your friends know exactly how you feel?

If you think something is wrong with your dog, follow your instincts. More often than not you will be right, with the marvellous benefit that a problem is diagnosed as early as possible. Follow the procedures outlined in this book to help you, but never rely on a book alone for diagnosing possible injury or illness. If you are at all worried about your dog, see your veterinarian.

Dr. Bruce Fogle

HOW TO USE THIS BOOK

WHAT'S UP WITH MY DOG? is a complete practical guide to looking after your pet's health. The first section provides a guide to understanding your dog's behavior, observing its vital signs, preventing disease, and performing first aid. The second section consists of comprehensive symptoms charts that enable you to look up any physical or behavioral changes that your dog may be displaying and, by following the yes/no flow charts, to identify whether there is a health problem and how you should proceed to deal with it.

This heading tells you that you are in the *Symptoms Charts* section of the book.

Each chart deals with a specific, visible symptom.

The introductory paragraph explains the particular health problem.

In addition to the main symptom, you will be asked about any other abnormal physical or behavioral symptoms shown by your dog.

All questions can be answered with a simple yes or no, which will then take you to the next relevant box.

If your dog is displaying the general symptom, start here and follow the flow chart to diagnose your dog's problem.

A button will advise you what to do. When emergency action is required, a red button alerts you to the urgency.

Additional text gives useful advice on ways to help your dog and explains the problem more fully.

Self-help remedies and practical advice are given where appropriate.

Clear photography is used to illustrate the relevant symptom.

By answering specific questions, you will arrive at a possible diagnosis.

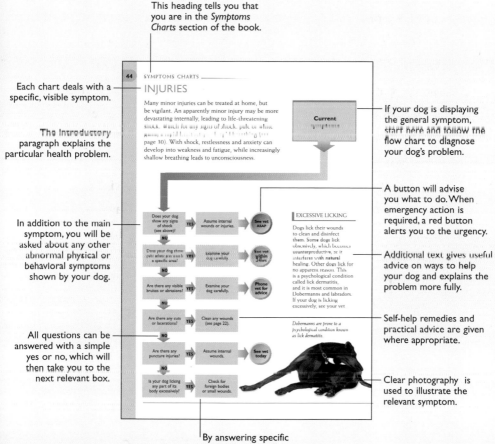

SYMPTOMS CHARTS

INJURIES

Many minor injuries can be treated at home, but be vigilant. An apparently minor injury may be more devastating internally, leading to life-threatening shock. Watch for any signs of shock: pale or white gums, a rapid heart rate, and rapid breathing (see page 30). With shock, restlessness and anxiety can develop into weakness and fatigue, while increasingly shallow breathing leads to unconsciousness.

Current symptom

Does your dog show any signs of shock (see above)?	Assume internal wounds or injuries.	**See vet ASAP**
Does your dog show pain when pressing a specific area?	Examine your dog carefully.	**See vet within 24 hrs**
Are there any visible bruises or abrasions?	Examine your dog carefully.	**Phone vet for advice**
Are there any cuts or lacerations?	Clean any wounds (see page 22).	
Are there any puncture injuries?	Assume internal wounds.	**See vet today**
Is your dog licking any part of its body excessively?	Check for foreign bodies or small wounds.	

EXCESSIVE LICKING

Dogs lick their wounds to clean and disinfect them. Some dogs lick obsessively, which becomes counterproductive, as it interferes with natural healing. Other dogs lick for no apparent reason. This is a psychological condition called lick dermatitis, and it is most common in Dobermanns and labradors. If your dog is licking excessively, see your vet

Dobermanns are prone to a psychological condition known as lick dermatitis.

PART 1
YOUR DOG'S HEALTH

Breed, sex, age, experience, and personality all affect
how a dog copes with injury or illness. To interpret
what's happening to your dog, it is important
to know how to examine it, and what to look for.
Understanding how to use life-saving techniques
prepares you to act efficiently and knowledgeably
when accidents occur and immediate action is vital.

DIFFERENT PERSONALITIES

The Yorkshire Terrier is a spirited breed, but it is often treated as much as a fashion accessory as a dog.

There are many different canine personalities, which is one of the reasons why we admire dogs so much. However, this also means that two dogs may react completely differently to the same event. These personality differences are highly individual but they are also, to a considerable extent, breed-specific. For this reason, you will gain a better understanding if you become familiar with the breed's personality traits.

Some dogs are stoic about life. They do not fret, even when genuinely ill. Others are complainers, whining and seeking comfort at the slightest disturbance to their routine or state of well-being. These dramatically different views of life are partly a result of selective breeding and partly a result of how we raise our dogs.

EATING HABITS

When I am assessing a dog, the breed matters, as different dog breeds have different eating habits. A Golden Retriever refusing its food, for example, is always clinically significant, while a Yorkshire Terrier refusing to eat may not be clinically important. Large breeds, such as the Golden Retriever, have a phenomenal rate of growth during the first year of life, and need huge quantities of food to survive. The litter size amongst larger breeds is also usually on the large side, and there is intense competition amongst puppies for the teats with the most milk. Natural selection and early learning both incline the larger breeds to gorge on whatever is available. I often describe the Golden Retriever, for example, as merely a life-support system for a stomach.

In contrast, Yorkshire Terrier puppies grow at a more leisurely rate, and produce litters half the size of Retriever litters. Genetically and environmentally, they do not have the same pressures to eat.

A final factor is you, the owner. People who acquire little dogs tend to think of them more as dependents. We often pander more to little dogs. These tykes quickly learn how to manipulate us, refusing perfectly good food when they know that something tastier is available.

VET'S ADVICE

BREED-SPECIFIC CONDITIONS

Read up on the health problems that occur with your breed or type of dog. For example, scratching in West Highland Terriers is often associated with allergy, coughing in mature Cavalier King Charles Spaniels may indicate heart disease, and diarrhea in Shetland Sheepdogs may be a symptom of colitis.

RESPONSES TO PAIN

Pain is a perception. There are no specific pain pathways in the nervous system. Vets know that the perception of pain varies between individual dogs, and also between breeds. Breeds such as Staffordshire Bull Terriers or Neapolitan Mastiffs, which have evolved from fighting or warrior dogs, are less sensitive to pain than breeds that have been created solely for companionship, such as the Cavalier King Charles Spaniel. If I am told that a Staffordshire Bull Terrier has yelped when touched, I take it extremely seriously. If I hear the same about a Cavalier, it may or may not be clinically significant. To understand your dog's behavior, it is important to know its individual idiosyncrasies.

The Golden Retriever is an even-tempered, energetic dog. It is eager to please and usually good with children.

THE AGE AND SEX OF YOUR DOG

VET'S ADVICE

Take your dog for regular veterinary check-ups, especially if it is a geriatric. Your veterinarian will monitor your dog and be able to assess any changes in its condition.

Any physical or behavioral changes in your elderly dog should be investigated by a vet.

What happens to your dog is greatly affected by both its age and sex. Young dogs, for example, are much more likely to get up to mischief, so accidents such as poisoning, electrocution from chewing wires, or choking may be high on your list of potential problems. Female dogs may suffer from a variety of physical and behavioral conditions associated with their seasonal production of hormones.

BEHAVIORAL CHANGES WITH AGE

Dogs are now living longer than ever before, so geriatric medicine has become a speciality in veterinary studies. As your dog ages, it may slow down, its taste buds may change, and it may become more aloof or more clinging. However, if you have an older dog, do not assume that all changes in its behavior are a result of growing older.

Appetite and activity changes can also be caused by illness. It can be difficult to differentiate between changes that are age-related, such as cloudy eyes caused by the inevitable accumulation of connective tissue in the lenses (sclerosis), and changes caused by a medical condition, such as late-onset cataracts. If your older dog is not behaving normally, consult the symptoms charts in the next section of this book. If, after doing this, you cannot decide what is wrong, contact your vet. Elderly dogs benefit from twice-yearly preventative veterinary check-ups.

SEX MATTERS

It is important to understand and differentiate sex-related activity from illness in your dog. For intact male dogs, the presence of a female in season can have dramatic consequences. It is not unusual for a male to go off his food when he scents a female in estrus, and a perfectly housetrained dog may urinate indoors. The male may even develop gastrointestinal conditions such as diarrhea.

A female in season may also display behavioral changes that can be erroneously interpreted as illness, for example, groaning or moaning, drinking more, becoming picky with food, and changes in toileting habits. After her season, a female may become depressed, preferring her own company to that of other dogs or people. Her taste buds may also change. These are all normal sex hormone-related changes. However, similar changes may also indicate a life-threatening womb infection. If your dog is unneutered, observe her closely and get to know what is normal behavior when she is hormonally active. By doing this, you will be better equipped to under-stand when your dog is showing signs of being ill.

NEUTERING

The effects of neutering are dramatically evident. Neutered females live, on average, a year longer than unneutered females. Early neutering reduces or eliminates the risk of breast tumors, the female's most common cancer, and excludes the possibility of womb infection or cancer of the reproductive organs. Additionally, it prevents the twice-yearly hormonally induced production of milk and the behavioral changes associated with the female's estrus cycle.

Neutering does not prolong a male dog's life expectancy, but it does reduce the risk of prostate conditions later in life. It may also decrease aggression in your male dog, and make him less likely to fight with other male dogs. Neutering also reduces a male dog's instinct to mark his territory with urine and enhances his response to any form of training.

Refusing to eat is a common side effect of the female estrus cycle.

EXAMINING YOUR DOG

HAVE A PLAN

If you intend to examine your dog, first work out a plan.

1 Talk to the dog reassuringly while calmly approaching. Do not stare at the dog as direct eye contact may intimidate it.

2 Check the dog's expression to gauge its demeanor.

3 Stroke a relaxed dog under the chin and then slip a leash around its neck. If a leash is not available, use a tie or a belt instead.

To find out what's happening to your dog, you need to examine it. In order to do this, you must have control over your dog. This is normally a straightforward procedure, but there may be circumstances in which your dog is frightened or in pain, and reluctant to be touched. When restraining your dog, be firm but gentle. Use the minimum restraint. Too much restraint upsets a dog, making it even more uncooperative. Make sure you do not put yourself at risk of being bitten by your dog.

Practise examining your dog by including parts of an examination in basic obedience training. Command your dog to sit or stand, and then examine it. Don't try to do everything at once. This is far too boring for most dogs. Instead, carry out partial examinations, for example the head and neck, or the skin and coat, always rewarding obedience with food treats, praise, and petting.

Remember, if injured or frightened, even the best behaved dog may not let you examine it. Therefore, you need to know how to restrain a worried dog safely.

Approach your dog calmly and stroke it gently under the chin.

MUZZLING A DOG

If you are not completely sure of your dog, use a muzzle.

1 Using a pair of tights, a soft rope, or a tie, make a loop large enough to slip over your dog's nose.

2 Gently slip the improvised muzzle over your dog's nose, keeping your hands well away on both sides. Always let your dog know where you are.

3 Tighten the loop on top of the nose, then crisscross the ends under the chin, bringing them back behind the ears. Do not let the tightness interfere with breathing.

4 Tie the loose ends in a bow behind the ears.

5 Take great care. Dogs are clever and find ways of removing poorly fitted temporary muzzles.

If your dog is frightened or in a lot of pain, it may be safer to muzzle it. In the case of a strong or extremely agitated dog, it may be wisest to attach a collar and lead before attempting to muzzle it.

RESTRAINING DIFFERENT-SIZED DOGS

- **Restraining a short muzzled or very small dog**
  Wrap a towel gently around your dog's neck. This stops it bending its neck and turning to bite you. The towel can be pinned while you examine your dog.

- **Holding a large dog**
  Wrap your arm as far as possible around your dog's neck. This will leave your other hand free to examine the dog.

- **Holding a small dog**
  Gently, but firmly, grasp your dog's muzzle. Apply a little pressure against your dog's body with the elbow of your free arm while you carry out your examination with your other hand.

DEALING WITH AN ILL OR INJURED DOG

If your dog is ill, injured, or in pain, it may be frightened or simply irritable. Its natural response may be to bite. Approach any unwell dog carefully, even if it is your own dog. Use a soothing tone of voice and gentle movements. Do not stare directly at the dog. This may be seen as threatening and heighten the risk of a snappy response.

WHAT TO LOOK FOR

MONITOR WEIGHT

It is sensible to monitor your dog's weight. For small dogs in particular, it is very important that you have accurate weighing scales. A loss of 8 oz (250 g) might not sound like much, but to a small Yorkshire Terrier it is the equivalent of you or I losing 20 lb (9 kg). An unexpected weight change is a subtle sign that something is wrong with your dog.

See your vet within 24 hours if you note:

Weight loss and:
• Fever
• Lethargy
• Vomiting
• Diarrhea
• Lameness
• Changed appetite
• Altered drinking habits

Weight gain and:
• Lethargy
• Increased thirst
• Reduced appetite
• Dull coat
• Hair loss
• Shivering or shaking
• Vomiting

Understanding what is happening to your dog is partly passive, based on what you can see, smell, and hear for yourself. More knowledge is gained actively by what you discover when you examine your dog. From the time that you first acquire your dog, it is good practice to train it to allow you to make a thorough examination. Get to know your dog, understand its different moods and the way its behavior can alter. In this way, you will be more alert and responsive to changes when they occur. As you examine your dog, note down your observations. Keep a record of the results and take this to your veterinarian when veterinary attention is needed. Use the following as a guideline for your examination.

A HEAD-TO-PAW EXAMINATION

OBSERVE	RECORD
Observe your dog's behavior and responses.	Record any changes.
Listen to the sounds your dog makes.	Record any changes, and take action if necessary.
Watch your dog's activities and movements.	Record any changes, and take action if necessary.
Smell your dog all over.	Record any changes.
Monitor your dog's heart rate and breathing rate.	Record rates.
Check your dog's gums for color and capillary refill.	Record color and refill time.
Pinch the skin on the back of your dog's neck.	Monitor your dog's state of hydration.

A HEAD-TO-PAW EXAMINATION

OBSERVE	RECORD
Examine your dog's eyes, ears, nose, and mouth.	Record observations.
Examine your dog's head and neck.	Record observations.
Examine your dog's body and limbs, including its paws and nails.	Record observations.
Examine your dog's tail, anus, and vulva and breast tissue, or penis, scrotum, and prepuce.	Record observations.
Examine your dog's skin and coat.	Remove any foreign material and record changes.
Observe your dog's gastrointestinal changes.	Record observations.
Monitor your dog's toilet habits.	Record changes.
Monitor your dog's eating and drinking activity.	Record changes.
Weigh your dog.	Record weight.

WORDLESS COMMUNICATION

It is only a surprise to people who have never lived with pets that words are not necessary for communication between a dog and its owner.

The way in which we understand our animals is very similar to the way in which we understand children before they have learned to speak. Through instinct and then learning, we understand how an infant feels or what he or she needs.

In a sense, dogs are infants for life. With time, their ability to communicate how they feel and our ability to understand what they are telling us improves. With experience, it becomes easier to understand your dog's wordless communication.

As you develop a relationship with your dog, you will begin to know instinctively when something is wrong with it.

BASIC PROCEDURES

An unwell or injured dog may need to be given medicine that has been prescribed by your vet. Getting your dog to take its medicine requires a gentle but purposeful approach. Simply dropping medicine into the dog's food bowl does not guarantee that it will be swallowed. Never call your dog to you just to give it medicine, or it might become fearful each time it hears its name: it is much better for you to go to the dog.

GIVING MEDICINE IN TABLET FORM

Unfortunately few canine medicines are available in tasty, chewable tablet form. Some pills even have an unpleasant taste. Dogs can be clever at hiding tablets in their mouths, only to spit them out later when their owners are not looking.

1 Command the dog to sit. With one hand, open its mouth, gently but firmly, holding its mouth from above.

2 With the other hand, drop the tablet as far back as possible, over the hump of the dog's tongue.

3 Hold the dog's mouth closed and its head up slightly. Stroke its throat with your other hand.

4 When the dog swallows and licks its lips, this means that the pill has gone down. Always praise the dog when it has swallowed the tablet.

HOME NURSING

In most circumstances, an unwell dog will get better faster when it is cared for by people it knows, in its own home. You should provide your dog with a warm, dry, comfortable place and make sure it has free access to its toilet area. A dog will not always understand why you are doing something that seems unpleasant to it, but you must follow the vet's instructions. Nursing a dog back to good health should always be carried out as kindly as possible.

Holding your dog's head up, stroke its throat for a few moments so that it swallows the tablet.

GIVING LIQUID MEDICINE

An effective method for administering liquid medicine is by plastic syringe. Also, if a dog refuses to swallow tablets, they can be crushed, mixed in sugar water, and syringed sideways into its mouth. Cough syrup can also be given with a syringe.

Hold the your dog's head firmly but gently from below while inserting the syringe between its teeth.

GIVING EAR DROPS

If your vet has prescribed drops for an ear ailment, give them as quickly and carefully as you can, according to the instructions.

1 While holding your dog's head still, and with the ear flap laid back, insert the nozzle of the bottle in the ear in a forward direction toward the tip of the nose.

2 Without letting your dog shake its head, withdraw the bottle and drop the ear flap back into position.

3 With the palm of your hand, gently but firmly massage the dog's ear. This lubricates the entire ear canal with medication.

GIVING EYE DROPS

Eye problems diagnosed by your vet require a course of drops to be given at home. Always continue treatment for as long as directed.

1 Clean the area around the eyes, wiping away any debris or discharge with moistened cotton pads.

2 Gently restrain your dog and hold the eye open, bringing your hand to the eye from above and behind so as not to frighten the dog.

3 Squeeze the required number of drops onto the eye and allow the eye to bathe in the medication.

Hold the dog's mouth firmly from below to keep its head still.

Allow the drops to bathe the eye.

HIDDEN MESSAGES

Your dog's body temperature, heart rate, and breathing rate are important indicators of its current state of health. There are, however, three more clues, which are equally important, but often overlooked. These clues are: gum color, capillary refill time (the amount of time it takes for blood to return to your dog's gums after pressure has been applied), and the elasticity of the skin on your dog's neck. Each of these indicators can provide vital information about your dog's health. For example, a vomiting dog with normal gum color and capillary refill time is not an emergency. In contrast, a vomiting dog with red, blue, pale, or white gums is an immediate, even life-threatening, emergency. By regularly monitoring these signs, you are more likely to identify promptly when something is wrong with your dog.

VET'S ADVICE

PIGMENTED (BLACK) GUMS

If you have a dog with completely pigmented gums (a Chow Chow or Shar Pei, for example), check the color of the mucus membranes inside the lower eyelid, in her vulva, or in his prepuce.

CHECKING FOR DEHYDRATION

What does it mean if the skin does not snap back immediately?

Your dog may be dehydrated.	**See vet ASAP**
Your dog may be malnourished.	**See vet today**
Your dog may be elderly.	Natural age-related loss of elasticity makes dehydration more difficult to assess.
Your dog may be obese.	Tight skin makes dehydration more difficult to assess.

The elasticity of the skin on your dog's neck is usually a good indicator of its state of hydration. In a healthy dog, when you pull the skin on the top of its neck and then let it go (known as "tenting"), the skin quickly snaps back to its normal position. To test for dehydration in elderly or obese animals, feel the gums. Dehydrated dogs have dry, sticky gums.

CHECKING GUM AND LIP COLOR

What is the color of your dog's gums and lips? What does this mean?

The color of your dog's gums indicates how much oxygen there is in its bloodstream. Lift a lip and look at the color of the gums or lips. Disregard any black pigmented areas.

Yellow	=	Your dog may be jaundiced.	→	**See vet within 24hrs**
Blue	=	Your dog may be in shock due to lack of oxygen.	→	**See vet ASAP**
White	=	Your dog may have shock or blood loss.	→	**See vet ASAP**
Pale	=	Your dog may be in early shock, or it could have anemia or blood loss.	→	**See vet ASAP**
Pink	=	This is normal.		
Red	=	Your dog may have carbon monoxide poisoning or bleeding in the mouth.	→	**See vet ASAP**

CHECKING CAPILLARY REFILL TIME

How long do your dog's gums remain blanched after applying pressure? What does this mean?

When blood is circulating normally, slight finger pressure on your dog's gums blanches the area under pressure. When the pressure is relieved, the area instantly refills with blood.

4 sec	=	Your dog is in deep shock.	→	**See vet ASAP**
2 sec	=	Your dog is in mild shock or has blood loss.	→	**See vet today**
1–2 sec	=	This is normal.		
Less than 1 sec	=	Your dog may have high blood pressure.	→	**See vet within 24hrs**

DEALING WITH WOUNDS

If you need to visit your veterinarian with an ill or injured dog, make sure that it is comfortable during transportation, and that the journey does not make its condition any worse. Protect any wounds your dog may have with a temporary dressing. Be particularly vigilant if you think your dog has an internal injury as this is potentially more serious than any injury you can see.

When emergencies occur, try to telephone your veterinarian to explain what has happened, and to let him or her know that your are on your way to the surgery. This will give the veterinary team time to have everything ready for your arrival. Try to remain calm during your journey—panicking may result in dangerous driving, putting both you and your dog at risk.

 VET'S ADVICE

Watch closely for shock, especially if your dog has closed wounds that result from trauma. Shock is life-threatening. Treating shock, including the causes of shock, must take precedence over everything else.

SYMPTOMS OF A CLOSED WOUND

Closed wounds are less obvious than open wounds as the skin is not damaged. Your dog, however, may have considerable internal injury, and be in need of immediate veterinary assistance.

The symptoms of a closed wound include:

- Swelling
- Discoloration caused by bruising under the skin
- Pain
- Increased heat in a specific area of your dog's body

If you see any of the above changes, your dog probably has a closed wound, and you should telephone your veterinarian immediately for advice.

DEALING WITH A CLOSED WOUND

1 If your dog has a closed wound, apply a cold compress as soon as possible. Lay a dish towel on the area (to prevent the cold compress from freezing the skin), then apply a bag of frozen peas. Keep in place for 15 minutes.

2 Your dog may have broken a bone. Before taking your dog to the vet, make a lightweight splint with folded towelling. This will immobilize the injured area.

Applying a cold compress to the affected area will reduce pain and swelling (see step 1). However, if the dog becomes distressed, remove the compress.

SYMPTOMS OF
AN OPEN WOUND

Open wounds must be thoroughly cleaned to prevent infection. Check your dog carefully for an open wound–if there is little or no bleeding, the wound may not be obvious.

The symptoms of an open wound include:

- Increased licking or paying attention to a specific area

- A new scab on the skin

- A skin puncture

- A trace of blood on the skin

- Lameness

If you see any of the above changes, look for an open wound. If you find a wound, clean it (see flowchart on the right), and telephone your veterinarian for advice.

DEALING WITH
AN OPEN WOUND

1 If your dog has an open wound and it is not large, remove any obvious dirt, gravel, splinters, or any other foreign object with your fingers or a pair of tweezers.

2 Flush the wound with a little salt water, clean bottled or tap water, or 3 per cent hydrogen peroxide.

3 If your dog's hair is getting into the wound, cut the surrounding hair. Before doing so, lubricate the scissors with a water-soluble jelly. This will ensure that the hair sticks to the scissors and not to the wound.

VET'S ADVICE

DOS AND DON'TS
- **Do not pull large objects out of an open wound (for example, an arrow or a piece of wood) as this may cause uncontrollable bleeding. Instead, get help from your veterinarian as soon as possible.**
- **Do not use petroleum jelly. It is difficult to remove later.**
- **Do not rub any wounds. Rubbing may result in more bleeding or damage.**
- **Do not underestimate small wounds. There may be considerable internal damage.**

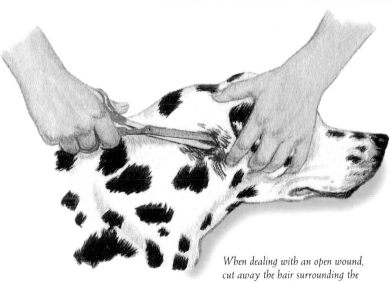

When dealing with an open wound, cut away the hair surrounding the wound (see step 3).

INFECTIOUS DISEASES

I have been in veterinary practice long enough to see numerous dogs die needlessly from infectious diseases, simply because the owners failed to vaccinate their pets. Inoculation can prevent a range of infectious canine diseases, and all dogs should be vaccinated against a core group of diseases. This core vaccination program will vary according to where in the world you live. How often your dog needs to be vaccinated will depend on the variety of vaccines available and the varying incidence of disease in different localities.

In addition to these core vaccinations, there are several other vaccines that may be beneficial under certain circumstances. Routine vaccination eliminates the need for you to worry about the variety of infections your dog may contract. Discuss your dog's vaccination program with your veterinarian.

DISEASE	SYMPTOMS	VACCINATION
Bordetella Commonly known as kennel cough, this infection is especially debilitating in breeds with delicate windpipes and in elderly dogs. It is contracted directly from infected dogs or their secretions.	• Hacking, dry, non-productive cough • Gagging • Sometimes phlegm	This intranasal vaccine is effective for up to nine months. You should vaccinate your dog if it attends dog shows, goes into kennels, or if it plays with other dogs.
Distemper Distemper can be fatal, even if treated promptly. It is contracted directly from infected dogs or their secretions.	• Coughing • Inflammation and discharge from the eyes • Vomiting and diarrhea • Fever and dehydration • Neurological changes, including fits, may occur later	• All vaccines are effective for a minimum of one year, many for longer. • Vaccinate puppies according to the manufacturer's recommendations, usually at eight weeks and again at 10–12 weeks of age. Boost one year later, then every one to three years, depending on what your vet advises.

DISEASE | SYMPTOMS | VACCINATION

Hepatitis
Hepatitis can be fatal if not treated promptly. It is contracted directly from infected dogs or their secretions.

- Vomiting and diarrhea
- Dehydration
- Jaundice

- All vaccines are effective for a minimum of one year, many for longer.
- Vaccinate puppies according to the manufacturer's recommendations, usually at eight weeks and again at 10–12 weeks of age. Boost one year later, then every one to three years, depending on what your vet advises.

Leptospirosis
Leptospirosis is transmitted in the urine of a wide variety of wild and domestic species, including rats. It is often contracted from swimming in contaminated water. It can be transmitted to people.

- Lethargy
- Loss of appetite
- Kidney problems
- Liver problems

- If your dog risks exposure to rat urine, vaccinate in conjunction with distemper.
- Give yearly boosters.

Lyme Disease
Early treatment with an appropriate antibiotic may prevent further signs of illness. Lyme disease is transmitted in bites from carrier ticks.

- Sudden lameness
- Joint pain
- Fever
- Loss of appetite

- Treat your dog for ticks regularly if exposed.

Parainfluenza
Parainfluenza is a mildly debilitating infection but it increases a dog's risk of pneumonia. It is contracted from infected dogs or their secretions.

- Coughing
- Retching
- Fever

- All vaccines are effective for a minimum of one year, many for longer.
- Vaccinate puppies according to the manufacturer's recommendations, usually at eight weeks and again at 10–12 weeks of age. Boost one year later, then every one to three years, depending on what your vet advises.

Parvovirus
Parvovirus can be fatal if untreated. It is contracted directly from infected dogs or their secretions.

- Severe vomiting and diarrhea, possibly with blood
- Lethargy and listlessness
- Dehydration

- All vaccines are effective for a minimum of one year, many for longer.
- Vaccinate puppies according to the manufacturer's recommendations, usually at eight weeks and again at 10–12 weeks of age. Boost one year later, then every one to three years, depending on what your vet advises.

Rabies
The symptoms of rabies vary enormously. Rabies is transmitted in the saliva of dogs and other infected animals. The disease is invariably fatal and highly contagious to people.

- Increased salivating
- Increased aggression
- Increased docility
- Paralysis
- Lameness

- Most vaccines are effective for two or more years.
- Vaccinate at 13–15 weeks, one year later, then every two or three years, depending what your vet advises and local law.
- Some places require annual vaccination even though the vaccine offers protection for much longer. Check on the regulations where you live, as well as in countries that you plan to visit.

EXTERNAL PARASITES

Some parasites, such as ticks, fleas, and lice, are visible on your dog's coat, while others, including mites, yeast, and fungi, are hidden to the naked eye. Parasites may cause a dull, dandruffy coat, inflamed skin without itchiness, or itchiness with or without inflammation. As well as causing skin conditions, external parasites may also transmit a variety of serious, even life-threatening, illnesses such as Lyme disease (see page 25).

Advances in safe external parasite control mean that there is no reason for any dog to suffer from skin parasites. Even so, parasitic skin conditions are still commonly diagnosed by veterinarians.

Current symptoms

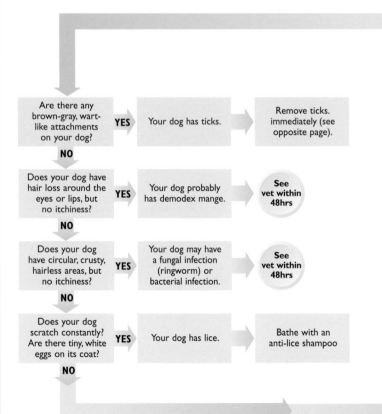

Are there any brown-gray, wart-like attachments on your dog? **YES** Your dog has ticks. Remove ticks. immediately (see opposite page).

NO

Does your dog have hair loss around the eyes or lips, but no itchiness? **YES** Your dog probably has demodex mange. See vet within 48hrs

NO

Does your dog have circular, crusty, hairless areas, but no itchiness? **YES** Your dog may have a fungal infection (ringworm) or bacterial infection. See vet within 48hrs

NO

Does your dog scratch constantly? Are there tiny, white eggs on its coat? **YES** Your dog has lice. Bathe with an anti-lice shampoo

NO

HOW TO DE-FLEA YOUR DOG AND YOUR HOME

Flea birth control

Use lufenuron, either a spot-on liquid or injection, on your dog. Any flea that feeds from your dog is effectively sterilized. Adult fleas then die off and your dog and home are cleansed of fleas.

This is a good product but it is not suitable for dogs who are allergic to flea saliva. For these dogs the fleas must be killed before they bite.

Flea killer

Use a topical product such as imidocloprid, fipronyl, or selamectin. Apply monthly as a drop on the skin of your dog's neck. Selamectin also kills roundworms, scabies, ear mites, and the American dog tick. Fipronyl kills ticks as well as fleas. All these products must be used in conjunction with a household biological spray that prevents flea eggs from hatching.

REMOVING TICKS FROM YOUR DOG

In areas where ticks are common, use a tick prevention such as fipronyl.

- If you see a tick attached to your dog, apply a tick spray, alcohol, liquid paraffin, or mineral oil to the parasite. This will cause the tick to loosen its grip.

- Using tweezers, grasp the tick as close to the skin as possible and rotate until it comes out of the skin. Avoid squeezing the tick's body as this sends toxins into your dog's skin.

- If a small black dot is left behind, you have missed the tick's head. Remove the head using a sterilized needle or tweezers. A plastic tick remover is available from your veterinarian.

- Ask your vet about locally transmitted tick diseases in areas you plan to visit.

HUMANS AND PARASITES

Some parasites affect humans:

- Fleas and ticks are as at home on humans as on dogs.

- Scabies and mites can irritate and inflame human skin.

- Ringworm is highly contagious. It can be passed from dogs to people, and vice versa. Immune-compromised people are especially at risk of infection.

PRACTICAL TIP

After vacuuming your home, dispose of the vacuum bag, as it may contain flea eggs.

Is there intense itchiness, especially around the elbows and ears? **YES** → Your dog may have scabies. → See vet within 24hrs

NO ↓

Does your dog have general itchiness? **YES** → Your dog may have fleas, malassezia yeast allergy, or another allergy. → See vet within 24hrs

NO ↓

Can you see fleas or flea dirt in its coat? **YES** → Treat your dog and household with an effective flea controller.

If your dog is constantly scratching, inspect its coat for any signs of fleas.

INTERNAL PARASITES

While some internal parasites cause obvious symptoms, such as vomiting, not all do. Therefore, some parasitic illnesses do not become apparent until considerable damage has occurred. Fortunately, most internal parasite infestations are preventable through routine worming.

Current symptoms

Does your puppy have a pot belly, hiccups, and a dull coat? **YES** Possible roundworms. → Treat your dog with an effective wormer.

NO

Has your healthy puppy vomited thin round-worms or passed them with diarrhea? **YES** Your dog has roundworms. → Treat your dog with an effective wormer.

NO

Is there rice grain-sized material in the fur around the anus? **YES** Your dog has tapeworms. → Treat your dog with an effective tapeworm drug.

NO

Is your dog dragging its bottom on the carpet or grass? **YES** Possible tapeworm, whipworm, or anal gland irritation. → Empty anal glands. Ask your veterinarian for guidance.

NO

Does your dog have diarrhea, perhaps with blood and anemia? **YES** Possible whipworms or hookworms. → **See vet within 24hrs**

NO

Does your dog have intermittent chronic diarrhea? **YES** Possible *giardia*. → **See vet within 24hrs**

LARGE INTESTINAL WORMS

Roundworms are the size of small earthworms. Puppies usually inherit them from their mothers, either via the placenta or in the first milk. Roundworms are the most common worms that puppies get.

The most common tapeworm that a dog gets uses the flea as its intermediate host. When a dog swallows a flea, it rids itself of the flea but gains a tapeworm. A dog can contract more serious tapeworms by eating offal or animal carcasses.

Hookworms and whipworms are now uncommon in pet dogs, but cause serious illness, especially in puppies, where they are associated with anemia, which may be life-threatening.

Prevention and treatment
Treat your dog with an effective wormer. Veterinary licensed drugs are very effective against the most common worms, particularly praziquantel for tapeworms and roundworms, and fenbendazole for roundworms.

MICROSCOPIC INTESTINAL PARASITES

There are three important microscopic parasites that affect dogs.

- *Giardia* causes diarrhea in both people and dogs. It is contracted by drinking fresh water that has been contaminated by wildlife.

- *Babesia* is transmitted by some ticks in North America and continental Europe. The disease is fatal if not treated immediately.

- *Toxoplasmosis* is caused by a single-cell parasite. It seldom causes problems in affected dogs, but is transmissible, via contaminated cat feces, to humans. It is of particular concern to pregnant women and people with immune-compromised systems.

Prevention and treatment
Use a product such as fipronyl to control ticks and prevent *babesia*. To prevent your dog contracting toxoplasmosis, prevent it from eating wildlife. Use fenbendazole to treat a dog with *giardia*.

HEARTWORM INFESTATION

Heartworms are spread by mosquitoes. They occur in many regions of continental Europe and North America. If allowed to mature, worms clog part of the heart and the major blood vessels around the heart. This causes gradual weight loss, a persistent cough, and a reduced capacity for exercise.

Prevention and treatment
Heartworm is preventable. Seek your vet's advice about the incidence of heartworm where you live or in places you plan to visit. Follow your vet's recommendations for preventative medication. Treatment involves a complex course of drugs.

LEISHMANIASIS

Transmitted by sandfly bites, this potentially fatal parasitic infection occurs throughout the Mediterranean. In 2000, the disease spread through foxhound kennels in eastern USA, raising the worrying possibility of dog to dog transmission.

Prevention and treatment
Only female sandflies carry *leishmania*, and they only bite at night. If you visit an area where sandflies live, keep your dog indoors at night as a preventative measure. The illness is extremely difficult to treat, and in many countries no licensed drugs are available.

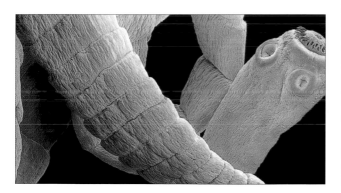

Dogs often host parasitic tapeworms (seen here magnified 16 times), and should be treated promptly.

RECOGNIZING SHOCK

In medical terms, the word shock refers to the body's response to changes in blood flow inside the body. Changes in blood flow occur when there is internal or external blood loss, major injury, anaphylaxis (severe allergic reaction), organ failure, or septic shock (circulating infection). Shock is insidious and can be a hidden killer.

LOCAL ALLERGIC REACTIONS

Dogs are fortunate. Insect stings and drug reactions are more likely to cause a reaction in the skin than a reaction in the lungs. When a skin reaction occurs, the muzzle often swells dramatically. The affected area is itchy, hot, and may be painful. Visit the vet for an antihistamine as soon as possible.

Your dog should then be monitored carefully for any symptoms of developing anaphylactic shock (see opposite page).

DIFFERENT FORMS OF SHOCK

Shock occurs when the body's cells do not receive enough oxygen—their main source of energy. This happens for three main reasons:

- Blood loss from external or internal bleeding

- Heart failure, leading to a lack of blood reaching cells

- Septic shock caused by bacterial by-products that prevent cells from using oxygen

If your dog shows any signs of shock, cover it with a blanket to prevent heat loss.

SYMPTOMS OF EARLY STAGES OF SHOCK

In the early stages of shock, the body compensates for the reduction in blood flow.

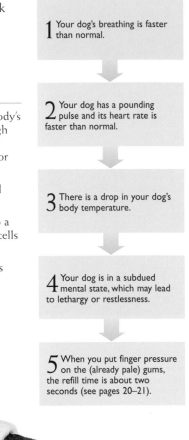

1 Your dog's breathing is faster than normal.

2 Your dog has a pounding pulse and its heart rate is faster than normal.

3 There is a drop in your dog's body temperature.

4 Your dog is in a subdued mental state, which may lead to lethargy or restlessness.

5 When you put finger pressure on the (already pale) gums, the refill time is about two seconds (see pages 20–21).

SYMPTOMS OF LATER STAGES OF SHOCK

If left untreated, shock can become life-threatening. The body can no longer compensate for blood flow changes, and your dog's body systems may become so overtaxed that they shut down altogether, resulting in death.

1 Your dog's breathing becomes slow and shallow, and its extremities feel cool to the touch.

2 Your dog's heart rate slows and becomes irregular.

3 Your dog's gums become pale or blue.

4 Your dog's mental state becomes extremely depressed, eventually leading to unconsciousness.

5 Your dog's pulse becomes weak or absent.

6 When pressed, the dog's gums take over four seconds to refill. **Heart failure and death are imminent.**

TREATING YOUR DOG FOR SHOCK

If your dog is in shock, treat the most urgent problems first. Stem any external bleeding, and give CPR if your dog is not breathing and its heart has stopped. As soon as your dog is stable, go to the veterinarian for professional help.

1 Do not give your dog anything to eat or drink, and do not let it wander.

2 Stop any obvious bleeding with finger pressure or a tourniquet (see page 46).

3 Keep your dog still, and wrap it loosely in a blanket to conserve body heat.

4 Keep your dog's hindquarters elevated with a pillow or towels. This encourages blood to flow to the heart and brain.

5 Give artificial respiration or heart massage as necessary (see pages 32–35).

6 Take your dog to the veterinary surgery. Ensure that the dog's head is extended during the journey.

ANAPHYLACTIC SHOCK

An insect bite, drugs, or, more rarely, a type of food can cause a dog to go into anaphylactic shock. Veterinary help is needed urgently. Your vet will give adrenaline by injection to counter the effects of this life-threatening allergic event.

Has your dog just had an injection, been given any medication, or has it been stung by an insect?

YES

Is your dog's face swollen? Is your dog retching, vomiting, or staggering? Does your dog have sudden diarrhea?

YES

Are your dog's gums blue? Is your dog showing symptoms of clinical shock?

YES

Your dog may be in anaphylactic shock. Keep your dog's airway open and give artificial respiration (see pages 32–33).

Is your dog making distressed gurgling sounds when it tries to breath?

YES

Your dog's lungs may be filling with liquid. Suspend your dog by its hind legs for 10 seconds to try to clear the airway. See the veterinarian as soon as possible.

IS YOUR DOG CONSCIOUS?

Before administering artificial respiration or heart massage, assess the condition of your dog by following these steps:

1 Speak to your dog. If it responds, then your dog is conscious.

2 If your dog does not respond, try pinching it hard between the toes. Watch its eyes carefully. Does your dog blink? If it does, it is conscious.

3 If your dog does not respond to either of the above, try pulling one of its legs. If it resists being pulled, it is conscious. A conscious dog does not need artificial respiration.

4 If your dog fails to respond to any of the above, it is unconscious. Emergency treatment is required.

5 If your dog is not breathing, but has a heartbeat, give artificial respiration.

6 If your dog's heart and breathing have both stopped, you should also use heart massage (see pages 34–35).

ARTIFICIAL RESPIRATION

Your dog's brain needs oxygen. If the brain is without oxygen, even for a few minutes, permanent damage occurs. Give artificial respiration if your dog's heart is still beating, but breathing has stopped. If the heart has also stopped beating, give artificial respiration and heart massage (see pages 34–35), together called cardiopulmonary resuscitation, (CPR).

To check whether your dog is conscious, pinch it hard between the toes and look at its eyes to see if it blinks (step 2).

WHEN TO GIVE RESUSCITATION

In humans, resuscitation techniques are commonly used to revive stroke and heart attack patients. Fortunately, these conditions are rare in dogs. However, your dog may need artificial respiration or CPR for the following reasons: smoke inhalation, choking, electrocution, near-drowning, heart failure, concussion, poisoning, blood loss, shock, or untreated diabetes.

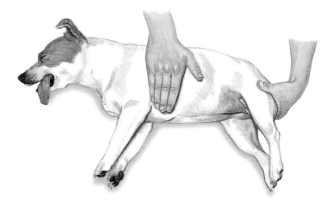

Check to see if your dog's heart is beating. If it has stopped (step 6), your dog needs heart massage, as well as artificial respiration.

GIVING ARTIFICIAL RESPIRATION

If your dog has stopped breathing, but its heart is still beating, start to give artificial respiration.

1 Place your dog on its side. Remove any debris blocking the dog's nose or throat. Pull the dog's tongue forward.

2 Close the dog's mouth. Wrap your hand around its muzzle to make it airtight. Then blow into the dog's nose until its chest expands. With small dogs, your mouth will seal its nose, mouth, and lips.

3 Take your mouth away and let the dog's lungs deflate naturally.

4 Repeat this procedure 10 to 20 times per minute. For small dogs, repeat 20 times per minute.

5 Check your dog's pulse every 10 seconds to make sure that its heart is still beating. Return to step 4 following this procedure.

6 If your dog's heart should stop, integrate heart massage with artificial respiration (see pages 34–35).

Clear any obstructions from the mouth and pull the tongue forward. The neck should be stretched forward.

Cup your hands around the dog's muzzle and blow gently into its nose. Try to keep the dog's neck straight.

BREATHING CHECKS

An unconscious dog may respire so gently that it is difficult to see its breathing. If you are not sure whether your dog is breathing, hold a mirror close to its nose and look for condensation, either fogging or tiny water droplets. If condensation is present, your dog is breathing. Alternatively, hold a piece of tissue or cotton batting in front of its nostrils and see whether it moves.

A-B-C

- Think A–B–C: Airway–Breathing–Circulation.
- Is your dog's airway open? If not, clear any debris and pull its tongue forwards. Be careful not to get bitten.
- Is your dog breathing? If not, give artificial respiration.
- Does your dog have a heartbeat or pulse? If not, give heart massage.

HEART MASSAGE FOR MEDIUM/LARGE DOGS

HEART MASSAGE

If your dog's heart stops beating, heart massage must be administered immediately. You must get the heart beating before attempting artificial respiration. To decide if heart massage is needed, apply finger pressure on the dog's gums to squeeze out blood. Does the blanched area refill? Check for a pulse. If you cannot find a pulse and the gums remain white, assume that the heart has stopped. As a final check, look at the dog's eyes—they dilate when the heart stops.

1 Place your dog on its side, with the head lower than the body. Place the heel of one hand on its chest, just behind the elbow. Place the heel of your other hand on top of your first hand.

2 Press your hands down and forward, toward your dog's neck, vigorously compressing its chest. Firm pressure is necessary to push blood out of the dog's heart toward its brain.

3 Repeat this pumping action at the rate of 100 times a minute.

Using the method described in step 2, begin heart massage at the rate of 100 pumps a minute.

4 Administer heart massage for 15 seconds, then give mouth-to-nose artificial respiration for 10 seconds.

5 Check frequently for a pulse. Continue CPR until you feel a pulse. Once your dog's pulse has returned, continue artificial respiration until the dog begins to breathe again on its own.

6 Get immediate veterinary attention for your dog.

Keep checking for a heartbeat while you give CPR. Once the pulse returns, continue giving artificial respiration only.

HEART MASSAGE FOR SMALL DOGS

1 Place your dog on its side, preferably with the head lower than the body. Grasp the dog's chest between your thumb and forefingers, just behind its elbows. Place your other hand on the dog's back.

2 Squeeze your thumb and forefingers firmly together up toward the dog's neck. Be vigorous, but not harsh. Do not worry about bruising your dog–this is a life-or-death situation.

3 Repeat this pumping action at a rate of 120 times a minute. Use a quick, firm pumping action.

4 Give heart massage for 15 seconds, then give mouth-to-nose artificial respiration for 10 seconds.

5 Check for a pulse frequently. Continue CPR until you feel a pulse. Once your dog's pulse has returned, continue artificial respiration until the dog breathes on its own.

6 Get immediate veterinary attention for your dog.

FLAT-CHESTED OR VERY FAT DOGS

1 If your dog is excessively fat or flat-chested, place it on its back instead of on its side. Make sure that the head is lower than the body.

2 Place the heels of your hands on the dog's breastbone. Press both hands down and forward. This pushes blood to the dog's brain. Be vigorous. Do not worry about bruising the dog unless there are rib or chest injuries.

3 Repeat this pumping action at a rate of approximately 80 times a minute. Use a quick, firm pumping action.

4 Hold each pump for a count of two. Release for a count of one. If you are pumping efficiently, you will feel physically exhausted within minutes.

5 Apply heart massage for 15 seconds, then mouth-to-nose respiration for 10 seconds. Continue CPR until heartbeat and breathing resume.

VET'S ADVICE

If two people are available, one should give heart massage, while the other gives artificial respiration.

If three people are available, make sure that someone calls the vet for advice. Then use the extra pair of hands to apply pressure to the dog's groin. This will divert maximum blood flow to the dog's brain.

PRACTICAL TIP

To check your dog's circulation, feel for a pulse on the inside of its hind leg.

PART 2
SYMPTOMS
CHARTS

For most dog owners, practical veterinary help is usually only a car-drive away. What is often difficult is deciding whether your dog's condition justifies the time and expense involved in a trip to the vet. In many situations, the need for medical attention is obvious, but the urgency is more difficult to determine. This section helps you to assess what's happening to your dog and when you should see your veterinarian.

CHANGES IN BEHAVIOR

Dogs use body language to tell us how they feel. The better you know your dog, the better you'll become at interpreting what it is telling you through its behavior. Some changes, such as hysteria, are obviously critical. Others, such as hiding, staring, or behaving in a subdued fashion, while not as dramatic, may indicate potentially fatal conditions such as shock.

Current symptoms

Is your dog distressed or in discomfort? **YES** → Does your dog appear to be in pain? **YES** → **See vet ASAP**

NO ↓

Is your dog hysterical or in a state of panic? **YES** → Does your dog appear to be in pain? **YES** → **See vet ASAP**

NO ↓

Is your dog unusually subdued? **YES** → Your dog could be ill. → **See vet today**

NO ↓

Is your dog irritable? **YES** → Your dog could be ill or in pain. → **See vet within 24hrs**

NO ↓

Is your dog unexpectedly aggressive? **YES** → May be seizure, pain, head wound, infection, brain disorder, diabetic or behavioral problems. → **See vet ASAP**

NO ↓

RABIES

The clinical signs of rabies vary enormously but all involve behavioral changes. While the typical rabid dog becomes wildly aggressive, spreading the disease in its drooling saliva, other dogs may become uncharacteristically subdued. Other signs include limping, difficulty swallowing, or a paralysis of one or more limbs.

Dogs should be vaccinated for rabies at 3 months or older and revaccinated annually, biannually, or once every three years, depending upon the state law and the type of vaccine given.

While rabies vaccination for dogs is mandatory for all states, it is estimated that up to half of all dogs in the US are not vaccinated. Vaccinating your dog is therefore vital to ensure effective protection against rabies.

AGGRESSION

If your dog suddenly becomes aggressive, follow the steps below:

1 Protect yourself, other people, and other animals from bites.

2 Reduce sensory stimulation by eliminating noise and subduing light.

3 Once your dog has become calmer, speak soothingly and observe the response.

4 If your dog responds, give a gentle "sit" command and attach a lead to its neck. This gives you greater control if the dog becomes aggressive once more.

5 If your dog has not been vaccinated against rabies and you live in a rabies-endemic area, do not touch your dog. **Call your veterinarian immediately.**

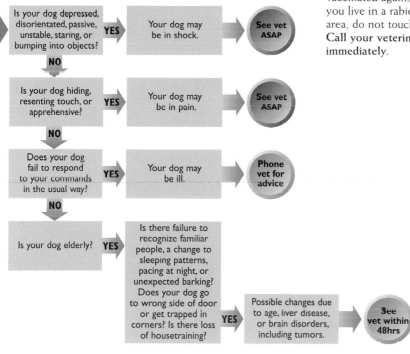

Sudden unexplained aggression may be an indication of pain or physical injury in your dog.

Is your dog depressed, disorientated, passive, unstable, staring, or bumping into objects? **YES** → Your dog may be in shock. → **See vet ASAP**

NO

Is your dog hiding, resenting touch, or apprehensive? **YES** → Your dog may be in pain. → **See vet ASAP**

NO

Does your dog fail to respond to your commands in the usual way? **YES** → Your dog may be ill. → **Phone vet for advice**

NO

Is your dog elderly? **YES** → Is there failure to recognize familiar people, a change to sleeping patterns, pacing at night, or unexpected barking? Does your dog go to wrong side of door or get trapped in corners? Is there loss of housetraining? **YES** → Possible changes due to age, liver disease, or brain disorders, including tumors. → **See vet within 48hrs**

LETHARGY

A distinct lack of interest in its owner or surroundings is an important indicator that a dog is unwell. If your dog appears depressed, or is unwilling to move around or play as usual, then it may be in pain or suffering from a serious internal disorder. As a general rule, if your dog suddenly becomes lethargic, see your veterinarian the same day.

Current symptoms

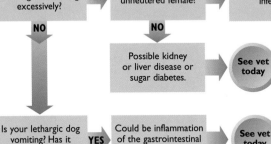

Is your dog lethargic and in apparent pain when touched or moved?	**YES** → Could be acute pain to joint, muscle, abdomen, or generalized pain.	→ **See vet ASAP**
NO ↓		
Is your dog lethargic and is its temperature over 103° F (40° C)?	**YES** → Could be possible infection or pain.	→ **See vet ASAP**
NO ↓		
Is your lethargic dog drinking or urinating excessively?	**YES** → Is your dog an unneutered female? **YES** → Possible womb infection.	→ **See vet today**

NO ↓   **NO** ↓

Possible kidney or liver disease or sugar diabetes. → **See vet today**

Is your lethargic dog vomiting? Has it got diarrhea?	**YES** → Could be inflammation of the gastrointestinal system or pancreas.	→ **See vet today**
NO ↓		
Is your dog lethargic, coughing and breathing with difficulty?	**YES** → Could be heart, chest, or lung disease (kennel cough, pneumonia, pleurisy, heart failure).	→ **See vet ASAP**
NO ↓		

WHAT IS PSYCHOLOGICAL DEPRESSION?

A depressed dog has lost interest in life. It is not interested in normal play, eating, or attention from people. While illness is the most common cause of depression, changes in a dog's lifestyle can induce a state of depression. Loss of routine, such as the loss of a family member, may induce depression in a dog.

Psychological depression responds to the same stimuli in dogs as it does in people–physical contact, attention, and play.

IS YOUR DOG DEPRESSED?

When a dog looks lethargic, we often interpret its behavior to mean it is depressed. If your dog is unwilling to play in its normal way, always eliminate medical reasons before assuming that there is a behavioral problem.

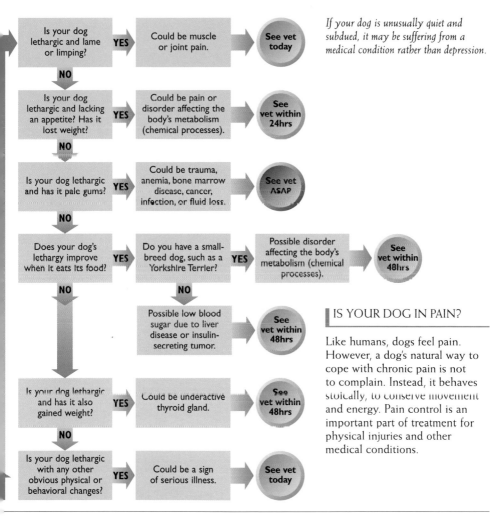

If your dog is unusually quiet and subdued, it may be suffering from a medical condition rather than depression.

Is your dog lethargic and lame or limping?	**YES** → Could be muscle or joint pain.	→ **See vet today**

NO ↓

Is your dog lethargic and lacking an appetite? Has it lost weight?	**YES** → Could be pain or disorder affecting the body's metabolism (chemical processes).	→ **See vet within 24hrs**

NO ↓

Is your dog lethargic and has it pale gums?	**YES** → Could be trauma, anemia, bone marrow disease, cancer, infection, or fluid loss.	→ **See vet ASAP**

NO ↓

Does your dog's lethargy improve when it eats its food?	**YES** → Do you have a small-breed dog, such as a Yorkshire Terrier?	**YES** → Possible disorder affecting the body's metabolism (chemical processes). → **See vet within 48hrs**

NO ↓ (lethargy) / **NO** ↓ (small-breed)

Possible low blood sugar due to liver disease or insulin-secreting tumor. → **See vet within 48hrs**

IS YOUR DOG IN PAIN?

Like humans, dogs feel pain. However, a dog's natural way to cope with chronic pain is not to complain. Instead, it behaves stoically, to conserve movement and energy. Pain control is an important part of treatment for physical injuries and other medical conditions.

Is your dog lethargic and has it also gained weight?	**YES** → Could be underactive thyroid gland.	→ **See vet within 48hrs**

NO ↓

Is your dog lethargic with any other obvious physical or behavioral changes?	**YES** → Could be a sign of serious illness.	→ **See vet today**

CHANGES IN SOUND

Listen to the sounds your dog makes—not only to its voice but also to any sounds its body makes. The sound of a dog's nails dragging when it walks, for example, may simply indicate they are overgrown, but it may also be a sign of joint or nerve conditions. Abnormal vocal sounds almost always indicate a serious problem needing same-day veterinary attention.

Current symptoms

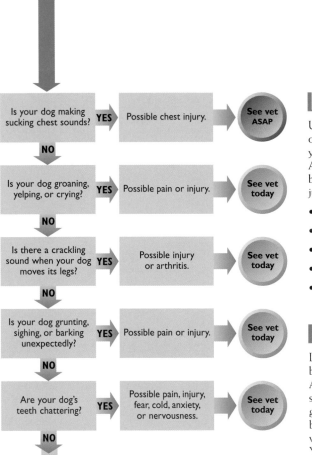

Is your dog making sucking chest sounds? **YES** → Possible chest injury. → **See vet ASAP**

NO

Is your dog groaning, yelping, or crying? **YES** → Possible pain or injury. → **See vet today**

NO

Is there a crackling sound when your dog moves its legs? **YES** → Possible injury or arthritis. → **See vet today**

NO

Is your dog grunting, sighing, or barking unexpectedly? **YES** → Possible pain or injury. → **See vet today**

NO

Are your dog's teeth chattering? **YES** → Possible pain, injury, fear, cold, anxiety, or nervousness. → **See vet today**

NO

SOUNDS AND ACTIVITIES

Unusual or changed sounds are often accompanied by changes in your dog's routines and activities. Abnormal sounds, accompanied by any of the changes below, justifies a same-day visit to the vet:

- Increased restlessness
- Increased sleeping
- Decreased sleeping
- Decreased alertness
- Decreased playfulness

BREATHING SOUNDS

Listen for any changes to regular breathing (see pages 72–73). An increase in harsh breathing sounds, snoring, wheezing, grunting, or sighing with each breath usually indicates a throat, windpipe, or lung condition. Your dog should be seen by a veterinarian within 48 hours.

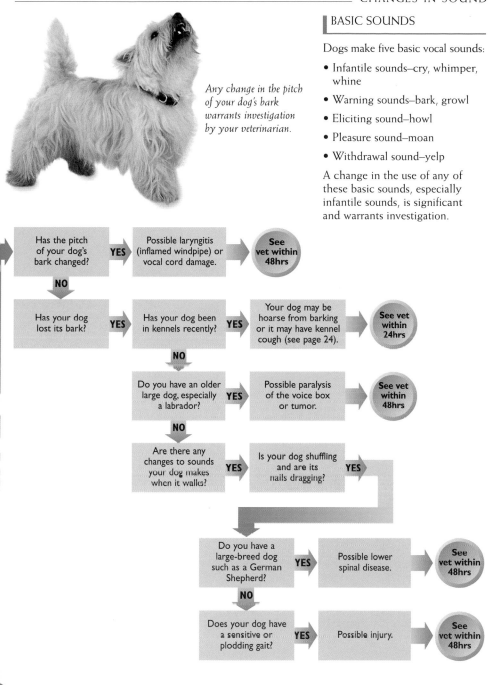

Any change in the pitch of your dog's bark warrants investigation by your veterinarian.

BASIC SOUNDS

Dogs make five basic vocal sounds:

- Infantile sounds–cry, whimper, whine
- Warning sounds–bark, growl
- Eliciting sound–howl
- Pleasure sound–moan
- Withdrawal sound–yelp

A change in the use of any of these basic sounds, especially infantile sounds, is significant and warrants investigation.

Has the pitch of your dog's bark changed? — **YES** → Possible laryngitis (inflamed windpipe) or vocal cord damage. → **See vet within 48hrs**

NO ↓

Has your dog lost its bark? — **YES** → Has your dog been in kennels recently? — **YES** → Your dog may be hoarse from barking or it may have kennel cough (see page 24). → **See vet within 24hrs**

NO ↓

Do you have an older large dog, especially a labrador? — **YES** → Possible paralysis of the voice box or tumor. → **See vet within 48hrs**

NO ↓

Are there any changes to sounds your dog makes when it walks? — **YES** → Is your dog shuffling and are its nails dragging? — **YES**

Do you have a large-breed dog such as a German Shepherd? — **YES** → Possible lower spinal disease. → **See vet within 48hrs**

NO ↓

Does your dog have a sensitive or plodding gait? — **YES** → Possible injury. → **See vet within 48hrs**

INJURIES

Many minor injuries can be treated at home, but be vigilant. An apparently minor injury may be more devastating internally, leading to life-threatening shock. Watch for any signs of shock: pale or white gums, a rapid heart rate, and rapid breathing (see page 30). With shock, restlessness and anxiety can develop into weakness and fatigue, while increasingly shallow breathing leads to unconsciousness.

Current symptoms

Does your dog show any signs of shock (see above)? — **YES** → Assume internal wounds or injuries. → **See vet ASAP**

NO

Does your dog show pain when you touch a specific area? — **YES** → Examine your dog carefully. → **See vet within 24hrs**

NO

Are there any visible bruises or abrasions? — **YES** → Examine your dog carefully. → **Phone vet for advice**

NO

Are there any cuts or lacerations? — **YES** → Clean any wounds (see pages 22–23).

NO

Are there any puncture injuries? — **YES** → Assume internal wounds. → **See vet today**

NO

Is your dog licking any part of its body excessively? — **YES** → Check for foreign bodies or small wounds.

EXCESSIVE LICKING

Dogs lick their wounds to clean and disinfect them. Some dogs lick obsessively, which becomes counterproductive, as it interferes with natural healing. Other dogs lick for no apparent reason. This is a psychological condition called lick dermatitis, and it is most common in Dobermanns and labradors. If your dog is licking excessively, see your vet.

Dobermans are prone to a psychological condition known as lick dermatitis.

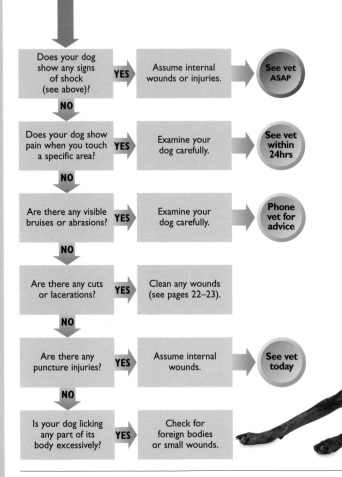

DOG BITES

Even the best trained dog may at some time be involved in a fight with another dog. Dog bites occur most frequently around the neck, face, ears, and chest.

Canine teeth can inflict deep puncture wounds, causing considerable soft-tissue damage under the skin. If your dog has a puncture wound, clean the wound and then take it to the veterinarian for antibiotic treatment.

If your dog has been involved in a fight, wait for it to calm down, examine it carefully, and then follow the steps below.

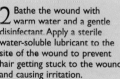

1 Check to see whether your dog's skin has been lacerated or punctured. If you can see a puncture wound, trim the hair surrounding the wound.

2 Bathe the wound with warm water and a gentle disinfectant. Apply a sterile water-soluble lubricant to the site of the wound to prevent hair getting stuck to the wound and causing irritation.

3 If the skin is lacerated, apply antiseptic cream to the affected area.

INSECT BITES

Wasp, hornet, and bee stings cause pain and swelling. Bees usually leave a sting embedded in the skin. To see if a sting is present, use a magnifying glass. If a sting is visible, remove it with tweezers.

Some dogs have an allergic reaction to an insect bite and go into shock. With this form of shock, known as anaphylactic shock, there is allergic swelling of the air passages. This causes the dog to make moist, gurgling sounds while trying to breath.

Administering adrenaline by injection is essential to stop anaphylactic shock.

Keep your dog's airway open and get immediate veterinary assistance for your pet (see page 31).

SNAKE BITES

Snakes (rattlers, copperheads, and cottonmouths in the US, and rattlesnakes in Canada) bite dogs more frequently than they bite people.

The signs of a poisonous snake bite are: trembling, excitement, vomiting, collapse, drooling saliva, and dilated pupils. If your dog is bitten, use a bandage to wrap a cold compress around the affected limb, and take your dog to a local veterinarian as soon as possible.

BLEEDING

External bleeding is simple to monitor. Minor wounds should stop bleeding within five minutes after applying simple pressure. Blood spurting can indicate a cut artery, however, which is often difficult to control. Any wound that bleeds for longer than five minutes needs urgent veterinary attention. Internal bleeding is more difficult to assess and can create a serious emergency.

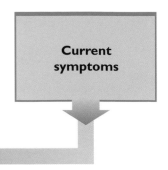

Current symptoms

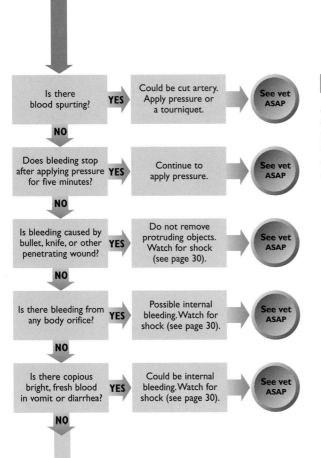

Is there blood spurting? **YES** → Could be cut artery. Apply pressure or a tourniquet. → See vet ASAP

NO

Does bleeding stop after applying pressure for five minutes? **YES** → Continue to apply pressure. → See vet ASAP

NO

Is bleeding caused by bullet, knife, or other penetrating wound? **YES** → Do not remove protruding objects. Watch for shock (see page 30). → See vet ASAP

NO

Is there bleeding from any body orifice? **YES** → Possible internal bleeding. Watch for shock (see page 30). → See vet ASAP

NO

Is there copious bright, fresh blood in vomit or diarrhea? **YES** → Could be internal bleeding. Watch for shock (see page 30). → See vet ASAP

NO

TOURNIQUETS

Always try to stop bleeding by applying pressure. If this is not possible or is not successful, and you are not within reach of veterinary attention, apply a tourniquet to a limb wound.

1 Wrap a piece of fabric above the bleeding wound and tie a knot.

2 Slip a pen, stick, or other firm, slender object into the middle of the knot and twist until the bleeding stops.

3 Hold or tie down the object, keeping the bandage firm and tight.

Be aware that tourniquets are dangerous as they cut off the blood supply. If left on too long, a tourniquet can cause irreversible damage to the limb.

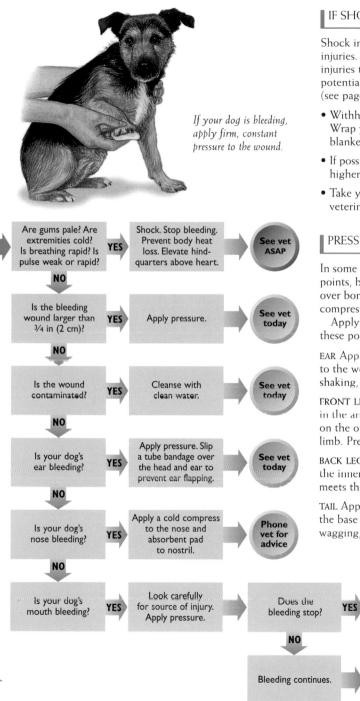

If your dog is bleeding, apply firm, constant pressure to the wound.

IF SHOCK DEVELOPS

Shock indicates hidden, deeper injuries. Both shock and the injuries that caused it are potentially fatal if not treated (see page 30):

- Withhold all food and drink. Wrap your dog in a warm blanket.
- If possible, keep the hindquarters higher than the heart and head.
- Take your dog to the nearest veterinarian immediately.

PRESSURE POINTS

In some locations, called pressure points, blood vessels travel over bones, and they can be compressed by external pressure.
   Applying hand pressure on these points stops bleeding.

EAR Apply pressure directly to the wound. Prevent head shaking, which dislodges clots.

FRONT LEG Place three fingers in the armpit and the thumb on the other side of the bleeding limb. Press firmly.

BACK LEG Place three fingers in the inner thigh, where the limb meets the body. Press firmly.

TAIL Apply pressure under the base of the tail. Prevent tail wagging, which dislodges clots.

Are gums pale? Are extremities cold? Is breathing rapid? Is pulse weak or rapid? **YES**	Shock. Stop bleeding. Prevent body heat loss. Elevate hind-quarters above heart.	**See vet ASAP**
NO		
Is the bleeding wound larger than ¾ in (2 cm)? **YES**	Apply pressure.	**See vet today**
NO		
Is the wound contaminated? **YES**	Cleanse with clean water.	**See vet today**
NO		
Is your dog's ear bleeding? **YES**	Apply pressure. Slip a tube bandage over the head and ear to prevent ear flapping.	**See vet today**
NO		
Is your dog's nose bleeding? **YES**	Apply a cold compress to the nose and absorbent pad to nostril.	**Phone vet for advice**
NO		
Is your dog's mouth bleeding? **YES**	Look carefully for source of injury. Apply pressure.	Does the bleeding stop? **YES** → **Phone vet for advice**
		NO ↓
		Bleeding continues. → **See vet ASAP**

EYE PROBLEMS

Changes to your dog's eyes are usually noticeable, whether due to injury, disease, or infection. For almost all eye conditions, it is best to get veterinary advice. Symptoms that appear to be insignificant may well indicate potentially devastating conditions. Your vet or a veterinary ophthalmologist can make an accurate diagnosis, using specialist equipment.

Current symptoms

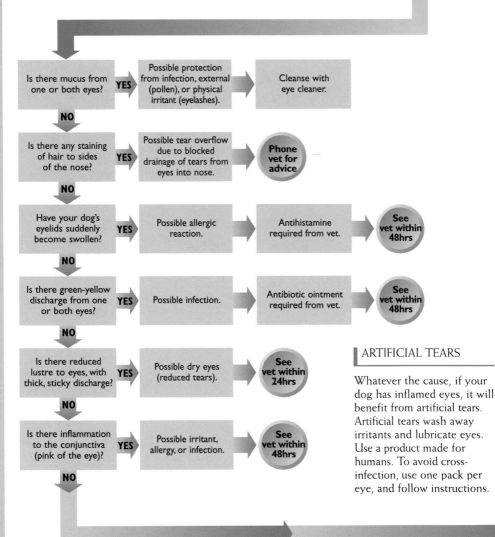

Is there mucus from one or both eyes? **YES** → Possible protection from infection, external (pollen), or physical irritant (eyelashes). → Cleanse with eye cleaner.

NO

Is there any staining of hair to sides of the nose? **YES** → Possible tear overflow due to blocked drainage of tears from eyes into nose. → **Phone vet for advice**

NO

Have your dog's eyelids suddenly become swollen? **YES** → Possible allergic reaction. → Antihistamine required from vet. → **See vet within 48hrs**

NO

Is there green-yellow discharge from one or both eyes? **YES** → Possible infection. → Antibiotic ointment required from vet. → **See vet within 48hrs**

NO

Is there reduced lustre to eyes, with thick, sticky discharge? **YES** → Possible dry eyes (reduced tears). → **See vet within 24hrs**

NO

Is there inflammation to the conjunctiva (pink of the eye)? **YES** → Possible irritant, allergy, or infection. → **See vet within 48hrs**

NO

ARTIFICIAL TEARS

Whatever the cause, if your dog has inflamed eyes, it will benefit from artificial tears. Artificial tears wash away irritants and lubricate eyes. Use a product made for humans. To avoid cross-infection, use one pack per eye, and follow instructions.

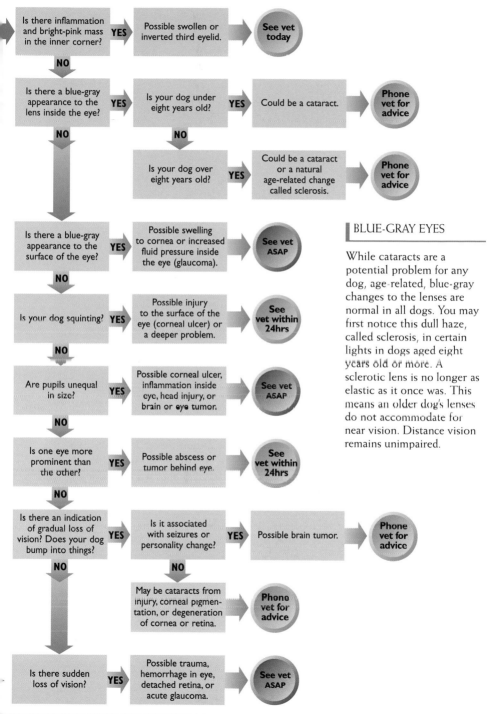

Is there inflammation and bright-pink mass in the inner corner? **YES** → Possible swollen or inverted third eyelid. → **See vet today**

NO

Is there a blue-gray appearance to the lens inside the eye? **YES** → Is your dog under eight years old? **YES** → Could be a cataract. → **Phone vet for advice**

NO

Is your dog over eight years old? **YES** → Could be a cataract or a natural age-related change called sclerosis. → **Phone vet for advice**

NO

Is there a blue-gray appearance to the surface of the eye? **YES** → Possible swelling to cornea or increased fluid pressure inside the eye (glaucoma). → **See vet ASAP**

NO

Is your dog squinting? **YES** → Possible injury to the surface of the eye (corneal ulcer) or a deeper problem. → **See vet within 24hrs**

NO

Are pupils unequal in size? **YES** → Possible corneal ulcer, inflammation inside eye, head injury, or brain or eye tumor. → **See vet ASAP**

NO

Is one eye more prominent than the other? **YES** → Possible abscess or tumor behind eye. → **See vet within 24hrs**

NO

Is there an indication of gradual loss of vision? Does your dog bump into things? **YES** → Is it associated with seizures or personality change? **YES** → Possible brain tumor. → **Phone vet for advice**

NO

NO

May be cataracts from injury, corneal pigmentation, or degeneration of cornea or retina. → **Phone vet for advice**

Is there sudden loss of vision? **YES** → Possible trauma, hemorrhage in eye, detached retina, or acute glaucoma. → **See vet ASAP**

BLUE-GRAY EYES

While cataracts are a potential problem for any dog, age-related, blue-gray changes to the lenses are normal in all dogs. You may first notice this dull haze, called sclerosis, in certain lights in dogs aged eight years old or more. A sclerotic lens is no longer as elastic as it once was. This means an older dog's lenses do not accommodate for near vision. Distance vision remains unimpaired.

EAR PROBLEMS

Head shaking and ear scratching are common dog activities that have various causes, both inside and outside the ear. Violent head shaking, often caused by a foreign object in the ear canal, may rupture a blood vessel and cause the ear flap to swell as it fills with blood. Some breeds, retrievers in particular, are prone to this condition, called a hematoma.

Current symptoms

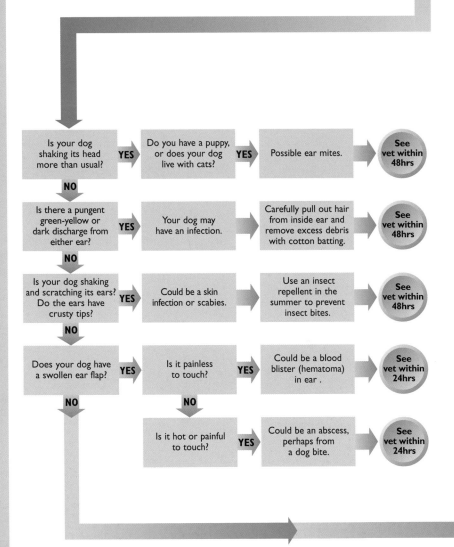

Is your dog shaking its head more than usual? **YES** → Do you have a puppy, or does your dog live with cats? **YES** → Possible ear mites. → See vet within 48hrs

NO

Is there a pungent green-yellow or dark discharge from either ear? **YES** → Your dog may have an infection. → Carefully pull out hair from inside ear and remove excess debris with cotton batting. → See vet within 48hrs

NO

Is your dog shaking and scratching its ears? Do the ears have crusty tips? **YES** → Could be a skin infection or scabies. → Use an insect repellent in the summer to prevent insect bites. → See vet within 48hrs

NO

Does your dog have a swollen ear flap? **YES** → Is it painless to touch? **YES** → Could be a blood blister (hematoma) in ear. → See vet within 24hrs

NO   **NO**

Is it hot or painful to touch? **YES** → Could be an abscess, perhaps from a dog bite. → See vet within 24hrs

ITCHY EARS AND ALLERGY

Veterinarians often see dogs with inflamed ears, itchy ears, infected ears, or smelly ears, but the ears themselves are not really the dog's primary problem. The condition of the ears is only the most visible manifestation of an underlying problem, which is allergy.

Allergic skin problems often start in the ears, which are one of the most sensitive and least protected parts of the skin. Treating only the ears, and not tackling the root of the condition, almost always ensures that the ear problem recurs.

DAMAGE TO THE EARDRUM

The eardrum is a delicate barrier, often damaged by infection or infestation. Once the eardrum has been penetrated, debris accumulates in the middle ear. It is much more difficult to clear a middle ear infection than an external ear infection.

If your dog has recurring ear infections, your vet will examine the eardrum to see if it is ruptured.

DEAFNESS, AND WHAT TO DO ABOUT IT

Most dogs cope well with deafness. If your dog is deaf, try the following:

- Use a lead. Deaf dogs are unaware of approaching danger, such as a car.

- Teach hand signals for simple obedience. Most dogs, at almost any age, quickly learn to respond to visual signals.

- Try a dog whistle. Some deaf dogs continue to hear this high-pitched sound.

- Be patient. Wake your dog with a gentle touch. Let it see when you leave. Think about getting your pet a canine companion who will act as its ears.

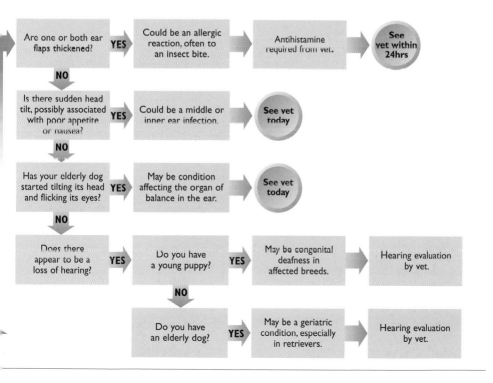

Are one or both ear flaps thickened? **YES** → Could be an allergic reaction, often to an insect bite. → Antihistamine required from vet. → **See vet within 24hrs**

NO ↓

Is there sudden head tilt, possibly associated with poor appetite or nausea? **YES** → Could be a middle or inner ear infection. → **See vet today**

NO ↓

Has your elderly dog started tilting its head and flicking its eyes? **YES** → May be condition affecting the organ of balance in the ear. → **See vet today**

NO ↓

Does there appear to be a loss of hearing? **YES** → Do you have a young puppy? **YES** → May be congenital deafness in affected breeds. → Hearing evaluation by vet.

NO ↓

Do you have an elderly dog? **YES** → May be a geriatric condition, especially in retrievers. → Hearing evaluation by vet.

SCRATCHING THE SKIN

There is always a good reason why a dog scratches itself, but sometimes it is frustratingly difficult to determine the exact cause. A consequence is that the itching gets treated rather than the actual cause of the itchiness. Parasites and allergies are the most common triggers that make a dog scratch itself. Scratching can often lead to secondary infection.

Current symptoms

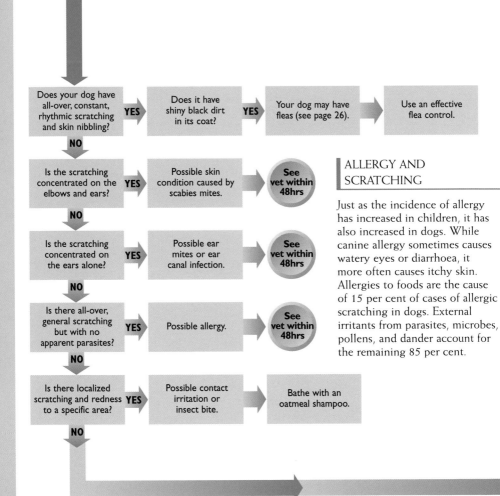

Does your dog have all-over, constant, rhythmic scratching and skin nibbling? **YES** → Does it have shiny black dirt in its coat? **YES** → Your dog may have fleas (see page 26). → Use an effective flea control.

NO

Is the scratching concentrated on the elbows and ears? **YES** → Possible skin condition caused by scabies mites. → **See vet within 48hrs**

NO

Is the scratching concentrated on the ears alone? **YES** → Possible ear mites or ear canal infection. → **See vet within 48hrs**

NO

Is there all-over, general scratching but with no apparent parasites? **YES** → Possible allergy. → **See vet within 48hrs**

NO

Is there localized scratching and redness to a specific area? **YES** → Possible contact irritation or insect bite. → Bathe with an oatmeal shampoo.

NO

ALLERGY AND SCRATCHING

Just as the incidence of allergy has increased in children, it has also increased in dogs. While canine allergy sometimes causes watery eyes or diarrhoea, it more often causes itchy skin. Allergies to foods are the cause of 15 per cent of cases of allergic scratching in dogs. External irritants from parasites, microbes, pollens, and dander account for the remaining 85 per cent.

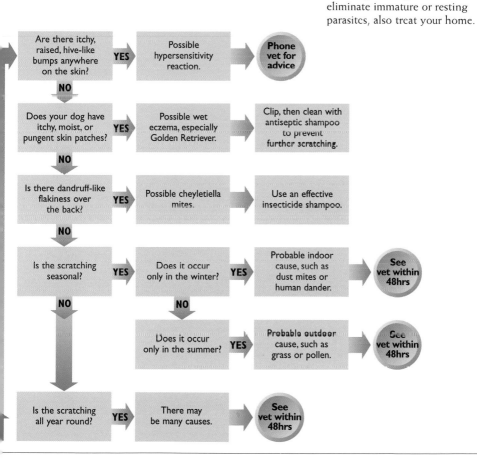

If your dog has an itchy or greasy coat, it may be necessary to use a medicated shampoo.

FLEAS

Fleas are the most common cause of scratching in dogs. Some dogs are irritated by the minute amount of anti-coagulant saliva left in the bite wound.

Bacteria or yeast may multiply on scratched skin and this may cause further scratching. The skin's oil glands become overactive, causing a crusty, foul-smelling condition.

You and your vet may never see the flea that triggered the chain of events.

If one of your pets has fleas, mites, or ticks, examine and treat all your dogs and cats. To eliminate immature or resting parasites, also treat your home.

| Are there itchy, raised, hive-like bumps anywhere on the skin? | **YES** → | Possible hypersensitivity reaction. | → | **Phone vet for advice** |

NO ↓

| Does your dog have itchy, moist, or pungent skin patches? | **YES** → | Possible wet eczema, especially Golden Retriever. | → | Clip, then clean with antiseptic shampoo to prevent further scratching. |

NO ↓

| Is there dandruff-like flakiness over the back? | **YES** → | Possible cheyletiella mites. | → | Use an effective insecticide shampoo. |

NO ↓

| Is the scratching seasonal? | **YES** → | Does it occur only in the winter? | **YES** → | Probable indoor cause, such as dust mites or human dander. | → | **See vet within 48hrs** |

NO ↓   **NO** ↓

| Does it occur only in the summer? | **YES** → | Probable outdoor cause, such as grass or pollen. | → | **See vet within 48hrs** |

| Is the scratching all year round? | **YES** → | There may be many causes. | → | **See vet within 48hrs** |

HAIR LOSS

There is a variety of causes of hair loss, not associated with itchiness and scratching. Some of these conditions are relatively insignificant, while others, such as autoimmune disease, may be life-threatening. The condition of your dog's coat is an accurate reflection of its health. Any obvious change warrants a same-week veterinary examination and diagnosis.

Current symptoms

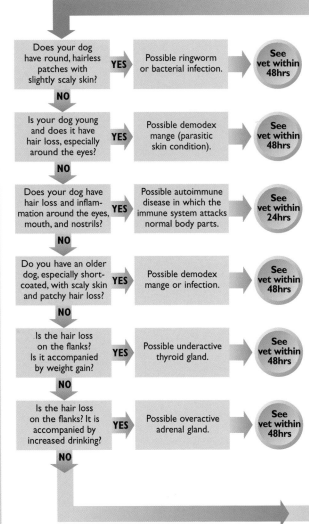

Does your dog have round, hairless patches with slightly scaly skin? **YES** → Possible ringworm or bacterial infection. → **See vet within 48hrs**

NO

Is your dog young and does it have hair loss, especially around the eyes? **YES** → Possible demodex mange (parasitic skin condition). → **See vet within 48hrs**

NO

Does your dog have hair loss and inflammation around the eyes, mouth, and nostrils? **YES** → Possible autoimmune disease in which the immune system attacks normal body parts. → **See vet within 24hrs**

NO

Do you have an older dog, especially short-coated, with scaly skin and patchy hair loss? **YES** → Possible demodex mange or infection. → **See vet within 48hrs**

NO

Is the hair loss on the flanks? Is it accompanied by weight gain? **YES** → Possible underactive thyroid gland. → **See vet within 48hrs**

NO

Is the hair loss on the flanks? It is accompanied by increased drinking? **YES** → Possible overactive adrenal gland. → **See vet within 48hrs**

NO

HAIR LOSS TO BLUE COATS

The color "blue" is really a dilute form of black, and resembles gray more than pure blue.

A genetic condition resulting in a "moth-eaten" partial hair loss to the blue portions of the coat may occur in the following breeds:

- Basset Hound
- Boston Terrier
- Chihuahua
- Chow Chow
- Dachshund
- Doberman
- Great Dane
- Greyhound
- Poodle (Standard)
- Whippet

HAIR LOSS WITHOUT A KNOWN CAUSE

Hormonal upsets may cause hair loss in a variety of breeds. However, some breeds, including the Dobermann, Boxer, Bulldog, and Airedale Terrier, experience a symmetrical and seasonal loss of hair on their flanks. The hair loss may be so drastic that they develop large dark-skinned bald patches.

Although the cause of this seasonal loss is still not understood, this hair loss is self-limiting. Hair usually regrows during the next hair-growing cycle.

WHY DOGS SHED THEIR COATS

A dog's coat generally thins during warm weather and regrows during cooler weather. Central heating upsets this natural rhythm, so many dogs shed their coats all year round. Some breeds, such as poodles, have coats that constantly grow, shedding little. Others, such as Yorkshire Terriers, have long outer coats and negligible undercoats, and these also shed little hair. Unneutered females often shed more after coming into season, during pregnancy, and while lactating.

Is the hair loss on the ears and nose (especially collies)? **YES** → Possible sunburn or solar dermatitis. → Use a sunscreen.

NO

Is the hair loss on the elbows? **YES** → Possible calluses on overweight or large dogs that lie on hard surfaces. → Provide soft bedding for your dog.

NO

Is the hair loss on the top of the tail of a male dog? **YES** → Possible infection or activation of a marking gland on the tail. → Clean with skin antiseptic.

NO

Is the hair loss at the base of the tail or on the flanks? **YES** → Probably self-inflicted or anal irritation. → Empty anal sacs. → **Phone vet for advice**

NO

Is your dog a neutered male? **YES** → Possible hormonal hair loss. → **See vet within 48hrs**

NO

Is your dog a middle-aged or older fine-coated breed, for example, a Boxer? **YES** → May be breed-related seasonal hair loss.

NO

Is there constant hair loss? **YES** → Does your dog have a healthy, shiny coat? **YES** → Natural shedding. → Brush to remove dead hair.

SWELLINGS AND LUMPS

Lumps and bumps are always worrying, but before you get needlessly concerned, remember that the majority of lumps are harmless. In some breeds, such as labradors, many mature individuals develop lipomas (harmless fat tumours). Cysts and abscesses are also common and easy to treat. Any lump should be examined by your veterinarian.

Current symptoms

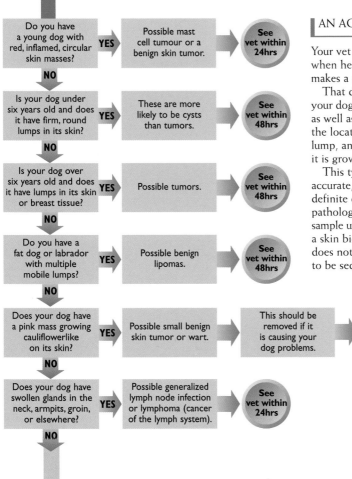

Do you have a young dog with red, inflamed, circular skin masses? **YES**	Possible mast cell tumour or a benign skin tumor.	**See vet within 24hrs**
NO		
Is your dog under six years old and does it have firm, round lumps in its skin? **YES**	These are more likely to be cysts than tumors.	**See vet within 48hrs**
NO		
Is your dog over six years old and does it have lumps in its skin or breast tissue? **YES**	Possible tumors.	**See vet within 48hrs**
NO		
Do you have a fat dog or labrador with multiple mobile lumps? **YES**	Possible benign lipomas.	**See vet within 48hrs**
NO		
Does your dog have a pink mass growing cauliflowerlike on its skin? **YES**	Possible small benign skin tumor or wart.	This should be removed if it is causing your dog problems. **See vet within 48hrs**
NO		
Does your dog have swollen glands in the neck, armpits, groin, or elsewhere? **YES**	Possible generalized lymph node infection or lymphoma (cancer of the lymph system).	**See vet within 24hrs**
NO		

AN ACCURATE DIAGNOSIS

Your vet makes an educated guess when he or she feels a lump and makes a diagnosis.

That diagnosis is based upon your dog's age, sex, and breed, as well as its medical history, the location and texture of the lump, and the speed at which it is growing.

This type of diagnosis is very accurate, but the only truly definite diagnosis comes from a pathologist, who looks at a biopsy sample under a microscope. Taking a skin biopsy is simple and often does not even require the dog to be sedated.

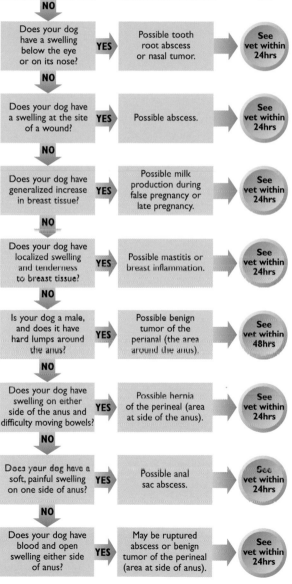

BREAST CANCER

This is the most common cancer in dogs. Spaying before the first season eliminates risk. Spaying during the first two years of life reduces risk. Spaying after this time does not affect the risk of developing breast cancer.

Tumors feed on female hormones. They have a surge of growth after each season.

TREATMENT FOR CANCER

The most effective way to treat cancer is to remove the lump surgically. If this is not possible, both chemotherapy and radiation therapy are sometimes used. Neither is as effective as surgery. When either of these therapies is used, it is employed at doses that do not cause a dog to experience side effects.

LAMENESS AND LIMPING

Lameness may be caused by something as simple as a bruised paw or something as significant as a broken bone. If your dog is lame, start by examining the paw and work up the affected leg. Take care: if your examination hurts your dog, you risk being bitten. The best therapy for all minor causes of lameness is two to three days rest, with exercise restricted to the lead.

Current symptoms

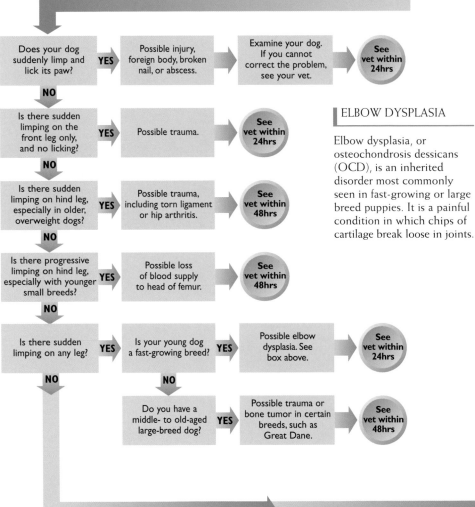

Does your dog suddenly limp and lick its paw? **YES** Possible injury, foreign body, broken nail, or abscess. Examine your dog. If you cannot correct the problem, see your vet. **See vet within 24hrs**

NO

Is there sudden limping on the front leg only, and no licking? **YES** Possible trauma. **See vet within 24hrs**

NO

Is there sudden limping on hind leg, especially in older, overweight dogs? **YES** Possible trauma, including torn ligament or hip arthritis. **See vet within 48hrs**

NO

Is there progressive limping on hind leg, especially with younger small breeds? **YES** Possible loss of blood supply to head of femur. **See vet within 48hrs**

NO

Is there sudden limping on any leg? **YES** Is your young dog a fast-growing breed? **YES** Possible elbow dysplasia. See box above. **See vet within 24hrs**

NO **NO**

Do you have a middle- to old-aged large-breed dog? **YES** Possible trauma or bone tumor in certain breeds, such as Great Dane. **See vet within 48hrs**

ELBOW DYSPLASIA

Elbow dysplasia, or osteochondrosis dessicans (OCD), is an inherited disorder most commonly seen in fast-growing or large breed puppies. It is a painful condition in which chips of cartilage break loose in joints.

TOXIC PAINKILLERS

Take great care if giving aspirin or ibuprofen to your dog. Both drugs often cause stomach irritation and remain in the dog's system longer than in ours. If your dog is one-tenth your weight, it needs a maximum of one-tenth the amount of painkiller you would take. Whenever possible, get veterinary instructions before using any over-the-counter painkillers.

FROZEN PEAS

Strains and sprains from over-exercise or rough play benefit from cold compresses, applied three or four times daily. A packet of frozen peas makes a practical and moldable cold compress. Place a cotton towel over the affected area (this prevents the area freezing), and then apply the cold compress. Leave in place for 10–15 minutes.

COUCH POTATOES

Not all dogs are natural athletes. Never ask your dog to do things that are not appropriate for its age, shape, size, or physical condition.

SLIPPING KNEECAPS

Because of an inherited anatomical fault, some dogs have unstable kneecaps that are prone to slipping off.

Breeds susceptible to this inherited problem include:

- Bichon Frise
- Chihuahua
- Jack Russell Terrier
- Maltese
- Pekingese
- Pomeranian
- Poodle (miniature and toy)
- Schnauzer (miniature)
- Spaniel (Cavalier King Charles Spaniel, King Charles Spaniel, and Toy Spaniel)
- Yorkshire Terrier

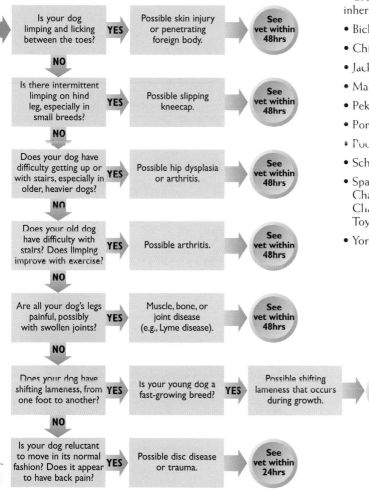

LOSS OF BALANCE AND COORDINATION

Balance is controlled by the semicircular canals in the inner ear and by the part of the brain called the cerebellum. Injuries, infections, inflammations, and tumors in these areas will make a dog unsteady on its feet, as can certain drugs. A head tilt usually indicates an infection in the inner ear, not a stroke. Strokes are less common in dogs than in people.

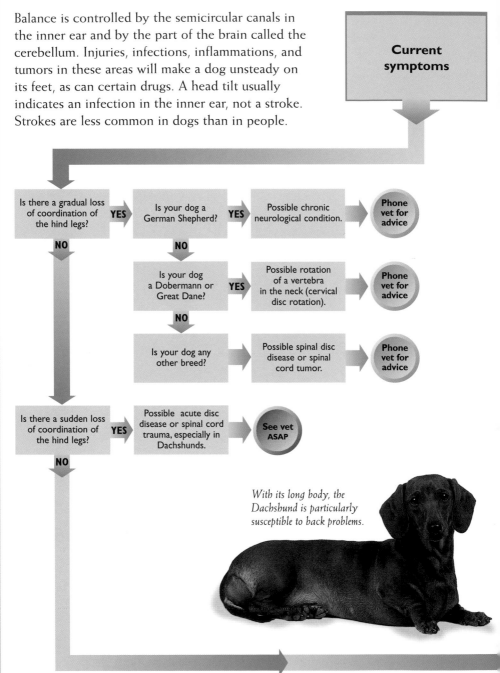

Current symptoms

Is there a gradual loss of coordination of the hind legs? **YES** → Is your dog a German Shepherd? **YES** → Possible chronic neurological condition. → **Phone vet for advice**

NO (from German Shepherd) → Is your dog a Dobermann or Great Dane? **YES** → Possible rotation of a vertebra in the neck (cervical disc rotation). → **Phone vet for advice**

NO → Is your dog any other breed? → Possible spinal disc disease or spinal cord tumor. → **Phone vet for advice**

NO (gradual loss) → Is there a sudden loss of coordination of the hind legs? **YES** → Possible acute disc disease or spinal cord trauma, especially in Dachshunds. → **See vet ASAP**

NO

With its long body, the Dachshund is particularly susceptible to back problems.

LOSS OF BALANCE

The signs of loss of balance include:

- Walking abnormally or falling down
- Circling in one specific direction
- A drunken appearance
- Head tilting to one side
- Rhythmic flicking of the eyeballs
- Vomiting

STROKES

Strokes are rare in dogs. Vestibular syndrome (VS) is a condition affecting the microscopic hairs in the organs of balance in the inner ear. Vestibular syndrome is commonly mistaken for a stroke.

The prognosis for a dog with VS is usually good, with significant recovery within a few days or weeks.

OTHER CAUSES OF LOSS OF BALANCE

Any condition that weakens your dog, for example, severe vomiting or diarrhea may cause a loss of balance. So, too, will chronic joint pain. Stumbling is often worst when a dog first gets up. A loss of vision will also cause a dog to appear to lose balance. All of these conditions demand veterinary attention and advice.

POISONING

If poisoning is suspected, immediate veterinary attention is required.

In the US, you can obtain advice from the ASPCA's National Animal Poison Control Center. Tel: 800-548 2423. A charge is made for this service.

Slug pellets are a common cause of poisoning.

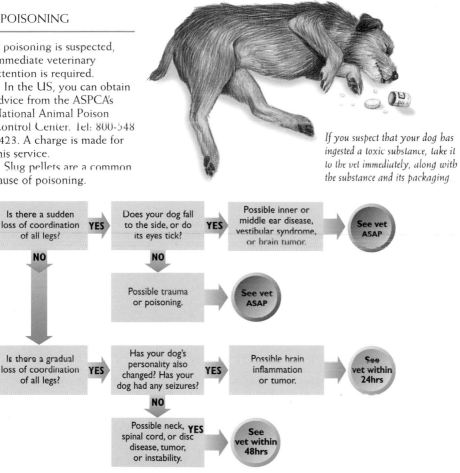

If you suspect that your dog has ingested a toxic substance, take it to the vet immediately, along with the substance and its packaging.

Is there a sudden loss of coordination of all legs? **YES** → Does your dog fall to the side, or do its eyes tick? **YES** → Possible inner or middle ear disease, vestibular syndrome, or brain tumor. → **See vet ASAP**

NO ↓ **NO** ↓

Possible trauma or poisoning. → **See vet ASAP**

Is there a gradual loss of coordination of all legs? **YES** → Has your dog's personality also changed? Has your dog had any seizures? **YES** → Possible brain inflammation or tumor. → **See vet within 24hrs**

NO ↓

Possible neck, spinal cord, or disc disease, tumor, or instability. **YES** → **See vet within 48hrs**

SEIZURES AND CONVULSIONS

At the onset of a seizure, a dog may appear confused, lose balance, or behave erratically. These symptoms often develop into a fit during which a dog may become rigid, paddle its legs, have tremors, urinate, defecate, or salivate. Some dogs lose consciousness. An episode usually ends within minutes. Dogs emerge disorientated, seeking comfort, and often hungry.

Current symptoms

COMA

A dog that is breathing and seems to be asleep, but does not respond to voice or touch, is in a coma. Comas are most common in diabetic dogs, but can also be caused by extremes of temperature, drugs, poisons, overwhelming infections, and shock.

ACTION Assess the possible cause of the coma and take your dog to a veterinarian as soon as possible.

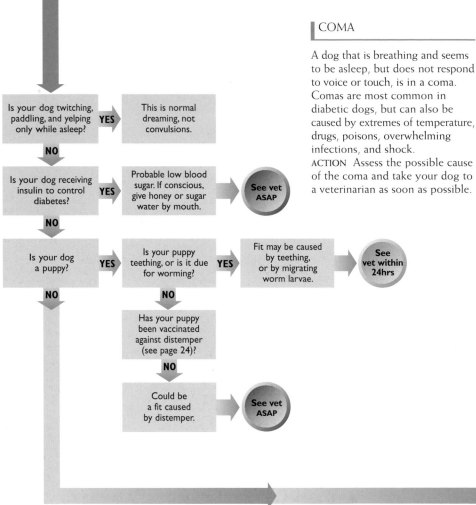

Is your dog twitching, paddling, and yelping only while asleep? — **YES** → This is normal dreaming, not convulsions.

NO

Is your dog receiving insulin to control diabetes? — **YES** → Probable low blood sugar. If conscious, give honey or sugar water by mouth. → **See vet ASAP**

NO

Is your dog a puppy? — **YES** → Is your puppy teething, or is it due for worming? — **YES** → Fit may be caused by teething, or by migrating worm larvae. → **See vet within 24hrs**

NO   **NO**

Has your puppy been vaccinated against distemper (see page 24)?

NO

Could be a fit caused by distemper. → **See vet ASAP**

Low blood sugar may induce a convulsion in a small-breed dog such as the Yorkshire Terrier.

CAUSES OF SEIZURES

Causes from outside the nervous system include:

- Liver disease
- Kidney failure
- Toxins from plants, animals, and chemicals

Causes from inside the nervous system include:

- Bacterial, viral, fungal, or parasitic brain infection
- Brain inflammation
- Brain abscess
- Brain tumor
- Brain scar tissue after a head injury
- Inherited brain abnormalities (birth defects)
- Low blood-sugar level

SEIZURES IN SMALL-BREED PUPPIES

Any stress, especially going without eating, even for a short period, can lower the blood-sugar level in small-breed puppies, particularly in Yorkshire Terriers. An affected puppy first appears weak and confused and may stagger. These symptoms quickly develop into sudden seizures or convulsions, often accompanied by profuse salivating.
ACTION Give honey, corn syrup, or sugar water at the first sign of weakness or confusion, and see your veterinarian as soon as possible.
Do not attempt to give anything orally to an unconscious or fitting dog.

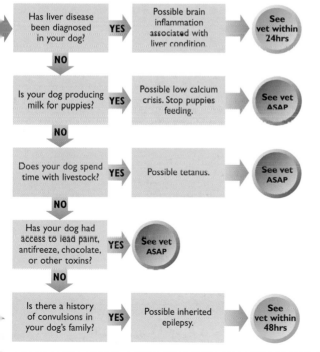

Has liver disease been diagnosed in your dog? — **YES** → Possible brain inflammation associated with liver condition. → **See vet within 24hrs**

NO

Is your dog producing milk for puppies? — **YES** → Possible low calcium crisis. Stop puppies feeding. → **See vet ASAP**

NO

Does your dog spend time with livestock? — **YES** → Possible tetanus. → **See vet ASAP**

NO

Has your dog had access to lead paint, antifreeze, chocolate, or other toxins? — **YES** → **See vet ASAP**

NO

Is there a history of convulsions in your dog's family? — **YES** → Possible inherited epilepsy. → **See vet within 48hrs**

CHOKING

Choking is an immediate emergency and should be differentiated from gagging, which may look very similar but is not life-threatening. If your dog is choking, do not wait for veterinary help. Instead, try to remove the cause of the choking. Be sure to take extra care—a choking dog may be in great distress and is liable to bite.

Current symptoms

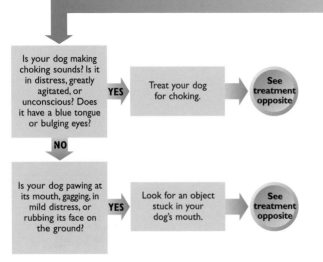

Is your dog making choking sounds? Is it in distress, greatly agitated, or unconscious? Does it have a blue tongue or bulging eyes?

YES → Treat your dog for choking. → **See treatment opposite**

NO

Is your dog pawing at its mouth, gagging, in mild distress, or rubbing its face on the ground?

YES → Look for an object stuck in your dog's mouth. → **See treatment opposite**

PREVENTING CHOKING

Dogs, especially puppies, will chew anything – as a natural method of investigation, to relieve boredom, to exercise the teeth and gums, or simply for the fun of it. Never leave small chewable articles where dogs can reach them. Puppies, in particular, swallow small objects and are at risk of choking on them.

OTHER CAUSES OF CHOKING

Swallowing objects is not the only cause of choking. An allergic reaction to an insect bite or a sting in the mouth may cause the tongue to swell. Physical injuries to the neck or throat may also cause swelling and choking. A dog can also choke on its own vomit. Seek immediate help from your veterinarian.

Dogs love to chew, but prevent choking by making sure that all toys are safe.

OBJECT IN MOUTH OF CONSCIOUS DOG

1 Gently restrain your dog without using a muzzle (see pages 14–15).

2 Open your dog's mouth with one hand grasping upper jaw and pressing upper lips over upper teeth.

3 With your other hand, open the dog's lower jaw.

4 Use a spoon handle to remove any object stuck on the teeth or in the roof of the mouth. Take care not to let object fall back into the throat.

CONSCIOUS AND CHOKING

1 Put your arms around the dog's belly, make a fist, and squeeze firmly up and forward, just behind the ribcage.

2 For a small dog, place both hands on either side of the belly and squeeze firmly up and forward.

3 Take extreme care when using your fingers to try to remove items from the throat of a conscious dog. The risk of being bitten is enormous.

UNCONSCIOUS FROM CHOKING

1 With the dog on its side, place the heels of both hands just behind the back ribs.

2 Press sharply to expel the blockage.

3 Use your finger to sweep any debris from the mouth.

4 If necessary, give artificial respiration and heart massage (CPR) (see pages 32–35).

5 If CPR is necessary, get immediate veterinary assistance for your dog.

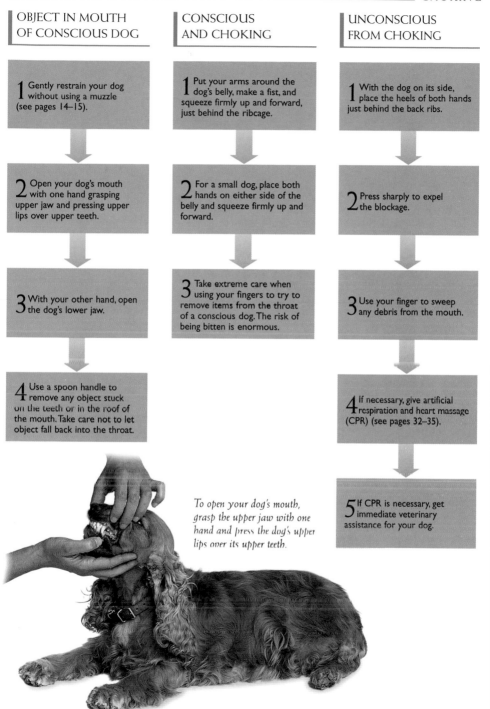

To open your dog's mouth, grasp the upper jaw with one hand and press the dog's upper lips over its upper teeth.

SNEEZING AND NASAL DISORDERS

A dog's healthy, slightly moist nose is prone to injury if it is used for rooting around on rough ground. Discharges and sneezing may be caused by minor conditions such as hay fever, or major problems such as nasal tumors. Sneezing is not an illness—it is a reflex action to rid the nasal passages of something the body considers to be irritating.

Current symptoms

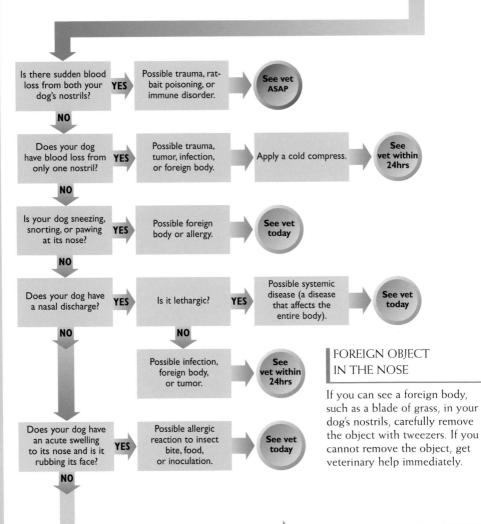

Is there sudden blood loss from both your dog's nostrils? **YES** → Possible trauma, rat-bait poisoning, or immune disorder. → **See vet ASAP**

NO

Does your dog have blood loss from only one nostril? **YES** → Possible trauma, tumor, infection, or foreign body. → Apply a cold compress. → **See vet within 24hrs**

NO

Is your dog sneezing, snorting, or pawing at its nose? **YES** → Possible foreign body or allergy. → **See vet today**

NO

Does your dog have a nasal discharge? **YES** → Is it lethargic? **YES** → Possible systemic disease (a disease that affects the entire body). → **See vet today**

NO **NO**

Possible infection, foreign body, or tumor. → **See vet within 24hrs**

Does your dog have an acute swelling to its nose and is it rubbing its face? **YES** → Possible allergic reaction to insect bite, food, or inoculation. → **See vet today**

NO

FOREIGN OBJECT IN THE NOSE

If you can see a foreign body, such as a blade of grass, in your dog's nostrils, carefully remove the object with tweezers. If you cannot remove the object, get veterinary help immediately.

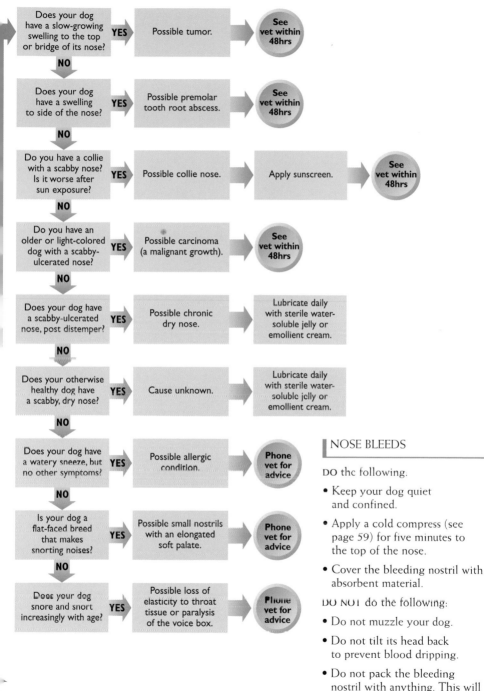

Does your dog have a slow-growing swelling to the top or bridge of its nose? — **YES** → Possible tumor. → **See vet within 48hrs**

NO

Does your dog have a swelling to side of the nose? — **YES** → Possible premolar tooth root abscess. → **See vet within 48hrs**

NO

Do you have a collie with a scabby nose? Is it worse after sun exposure? — **YES** → Possible collie nose. → Apply sunscreen. → **See vet within 48hrs**

NO

Do you have an older or light-colored dog with a scabby-ulcerated nose? — **YES** → Possible carcinoma (a malignant growth). → **See vet within 48hrs**

NO

Does your dog have a scabby-ulcerated nose, post distemper? — **YES** → Possible chronic dry nose. → Lubricate daily with sterile water-soluble jelly or emollient cream.

NO

Does your otherwise healthy dog have a scabby, dry nose? — **YES** → Cause unknown. → Lubricate daily with sterile water-soluble jelly or emollient cream.

NO

Does your dog have a watery sneeze, but no other symptoms? — **YES** → Possible allergic condition. → **Phone vet for advice**

NO

Is your dog a flat-faced breed that makes snorting noises? — **YES** → Possible small nostrils with an elongated soft palate. → **Phone vet for advice**

NO

Does your dog snore and snort increasingly with age? — **YES** → Possible loss of elasticity to throat tissue or paralysis of the voice box. → **Phone vet for advice**

NOSE BLEEDS

DO the following.

- Keep your dog quiet and confined.

- Apply a cold compress (see page 59) for five minutes to the top of the nose.

- Cover the bleeding nostril with absorbent material.

DO NOT do the following:

- Do not muzzle your dog.

- Do not tilt its head back to prevent blood dripping.

- Do not pack the bleeding nostril with anything. This will only cause the dog to sneeze.

COUGHING

Coughing is a natural reflex to remove unwanted material from the air passages. Coughing is also triggered by damage to the lining of the air passages. It may be caused by allergy, pollution, poisons, infections, worms, heart conditions, chest diseases or injuries, tumors, or a collapsed windpipe.

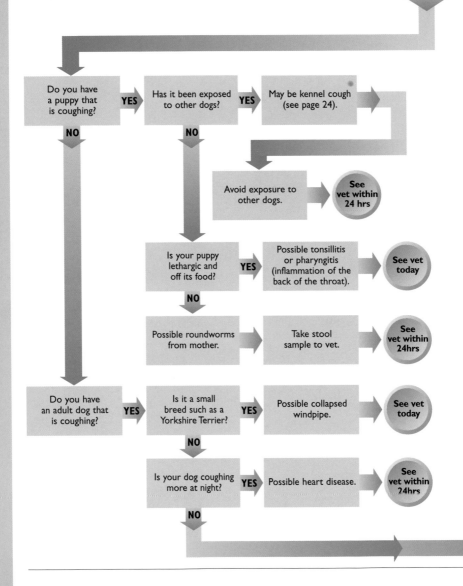

Current symptoms

Do you have a puppy that is coughing? — **YES** → Has it been exposed to other dogs? — **YES** → May be kennel cough (see page 24).

NO ↓   **NO** ↓

Avoid exposure to other dogs. → **See vet within 24 hrs**

Is your puppy lethargic and off its food? — **YES** → Possible tonsillitis or pharyngitis (inflammation of the back of the throat). → **See vet today**

NO ↓

Possible roundworms from mother. → Take stool sample to vet. → **See vet within 24hrs**

Do you have an adult dog that is coughing? — **YES** → Is it a small breed such as a Yorkshire Terrier? — **YES** → Possible collapsed windpipe. → **See vet today**

NO ↓

Is your dog coughing more at night? — **YES** → Possible heart disease. → **See vet within 24hrs**

NO ↓

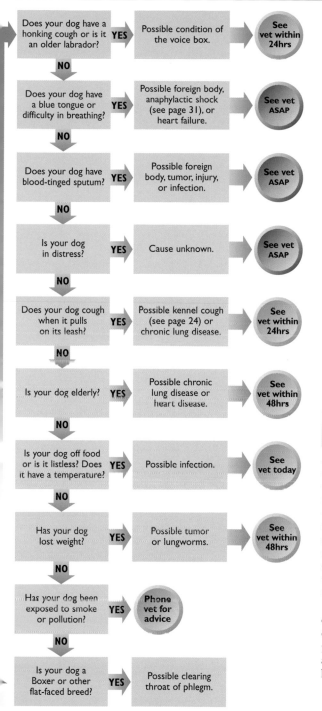

Does your dog have a honking cough or is it an older labrador? **YES** → Possible condition of the voice box. → **See vet within 24hrs**

NO ↓

Does your dog have a blue tongue or difficulty in breathing? **YES** → Possible foreign body, anaphylactic shock (see page 31), or heart failure. → **See vet ASAP**

NO ↓

Does your dog have blood-tinged sputum? **YES** → Possible foreign body, tumor, injury, or infection. → **See vet ASAP**

NO ↓

Is your dog in distress? **YES** → Cause unknown. → **See vet ASAP**

NO ↓

Does your dog cough when it pulls on its leash? **YES** → Possible kennel cough (see page 24) or chronic lung disease. → **See vet within 24hrs**

NO ↓

Is your dog elderly? **YES** → Possible chronic lung disease or heart disease. → **See vet within 48hrs**

NO ↓

Is your dog off food or is it listless? Does it have a temperature? **YES** → Possible infection. → **See vet today**

NO ↓

Has your dog lost weight? **YES** → Possible tumor or lungworms. → **See vet within 48hrs**

NO ↓

Has your dog been exposed to smoke or pollution? **YES** → **Phone vet for advice**

NO ↓

Is your dog a Boxer or other flat-faced breed? **YES** → Possible clearing throat of phlegm.

HOME TREATMENT FOR MINOR COUGHS

- Give veterinary expectorant, not cough suppressor. Follow instructions on the package, based on your dog's body weight.

- Increase environmental moisture with humidifier or steam in room.

- If there is no improvement in 36 hours, contact your veterinarian for advice.

SMALL SNORTING DOGS

Some small dogs, especially Yorkshire Terriers, will sometimes brace themselves and snort inward. It looks dangerous, but is usually an insignificant spasm of the diaphragm and does not require the attention of a vet.

VACCINATION AGAINST INFECTION

Although distemper no longer occurs with the frequency it once did, this preventable infection often causes breathing difficulties, including coughing associated with fever, lethargy, gastrointestinal problems, and nose and eye discharges. All dogs should be vaccinated against this potentially lethal infection (see page 24).

Dogs that are likely to have contact with other dogs, for example, during kennel stays or park visits, should be vaccinated against the variety of causes of kennel cough (see page 24).

BAD BREATH

Bad breath, or halitosis, is most often caused by poor oral hygiene and the build-up of bacteria associated with excessive tartar on the teeth. It can also be caused by mouth infections and, in older dogs, mouth tumors. Bad breath may also be a sign of more serious problems, including sugar diabetes, kidney disease, and a range of digestive disorders.

Current symptoms

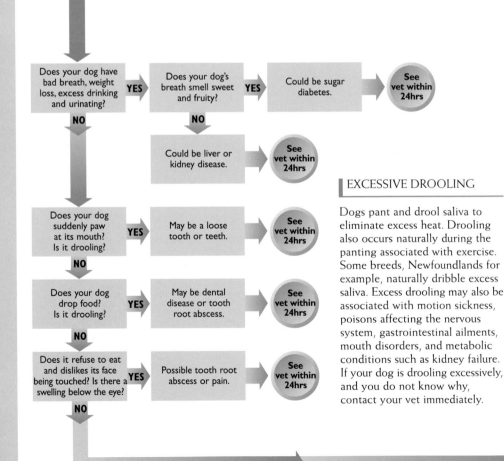

Does your dog have bad breath, weight loss, excess drinking and urinating? **YES** → Does your dog's breath smell sweet and fruity? **YES** → Could be sugar diabetes. → **See vet within 24hrs**

NO ↓ **NO** ↓

Could be liver or kidney disease. → **See vet within 24hrs**

Does your dog suddenly paw at its mouth? Is it drooling? **YES** → May be a loose tooth or teeth. → **See vet within 24hrs**

NO ↓

Does your dog drop food? Is it drooling? **YES** → May be dental disease or tooth root abscess. → **See vet within 24hrs**

NO ↓

Does it refuse to eat and dislikes its face being touched? Is there a swelling below the eye? **YES** → Possible tooth root abscess or pain. → **See vet within 24hrs**

NO ↓

EXCESSIVE DROOLING

Dogs pant and drool saliva to eliminate excess heat. Drooling also occurs naturally during the panting associated with exercise. Some breeds, Newfoundlands for example, naturally dribble excess saliva. Excess drooling may also be associated with motion sickness, poisons affecting the nervous system, gastrointestinal ailments, mouth disorders, and metabolic conditions such as kidney failure. If your dog is drooling excessively, and you do not know why, contact your vet immediately.

ORAL HYGIENE

Bad breath is the most obvious sign of poor oral hygiene but there are other more important consequences. There is evidence that gum disease associated with bad breath is directly linked to heart and kidney disease.

Gum disease, poor oral hygiene, and associated heart disease are more common problems in small-breed dogs. It is very important that small dogs, in particular, maintain good oral hygiene. Diets, toys, and games that exercise the teeth and gums promote good oral hygiene.

As with people, most dogs, whether small, medium, or large, eventually need and benefit from professional teeth scaling and polishing.

If your dog has bad breath, ask your vet to examine it to identify the cause.

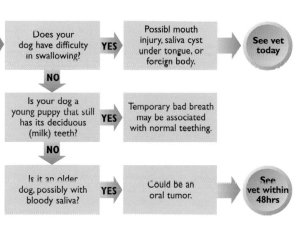

Does your dog have difficulty in swallowing?	**YES** → Possibl mouth injury, saliva cyst under tongue, or foreign body.	→ **See vet today**
NO ↓		
Is your dog a young puppy that still has its deciduous (milk) teeth?	**YES** → Temporary bad breath may be associated with normal teething.	
NO ↓		
Is it an older dog, possibly with bloody saliva?	**YES** → Could be an oral tumor.	→ **See vet within 48hrs**

ORAL TUMORS

Oral tumors may occur in older dogs, particularly short-nosed breeds such as Boxers, but also in spaniels and pointers. Short-nosed breeds also commonly develop a benign thickening of the gums, called an epulis. This condition, which can develop in younger individuals, can be a focus of bad breath. An epulis is usually surgically removed when a dog's teeth are scaled and polished.

BREATHING PROBLEMS

With most breathing problems, your dog will use its stomach muscles increasingly to get more air. Bacterial or viral infections involving the windpipe and lungs are usually obvious, but breathing problems associated with heart conditions may develop more insidiously. These problems are more easily dismissed as relatively unimportant, but they can be equally, or more, serious.

Current symptoms

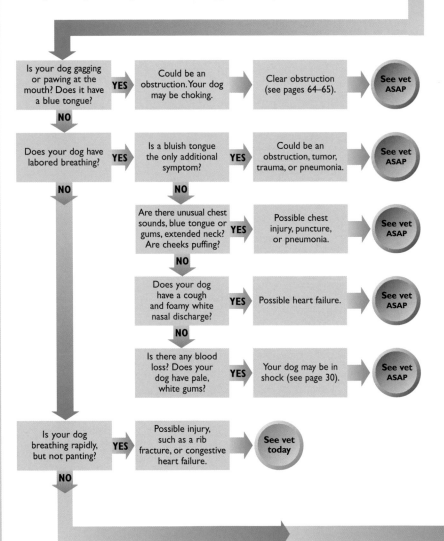

Is your dog gagging or pawing at the mouth? Does it have a blue tongue?

YES → Could be an obstruction. Your dog may be choking. → Clear obstruction (see pages 64–65). → **See vet ASAP**

NO

Does your dog have labored breathing?

YES → Is a bluish tongue the only additional symptom?

YES → Could be an obstruction, tumor, trauma, or pneumonia. → **See vet ASAP**

NO

Are there unusual chest sounds, blue tongue or gums, extended neck? Are cheeks puffing?

YES → Possible chest injury, puncture, or pneumonia. → **See vet ASAP**

NO

Does your dog have a cough and foamy white nasal discharge?

YES → Possible heart failure. → **See vet ASAP**

NO

Is there any blood loss? Does your dog have pale, white gums?

YES → Your dog may be in shock (see page 30). → **See vet ASAP**

NO

Is your dog breathing rapidly, but not panting?

YES → Possible injury, such as a rib fracture, or congestive heart failure. → **See vet today**

NO

PANTING

Do not mistake normal panting for labored breathing. Panting, which is shallow, rapid, open-mouthed breathing, is not a medical problem. All hot, nervous, excited, or exhausted dogs pant. Exercise induces panting, as will pain or even some medications, such as corticosteroids. Contact your veterinarian if there is any inexplicable panting.

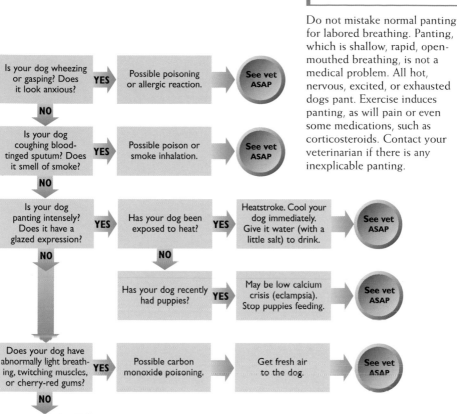

Is your dog wheezing or gasping? Does it look anxious? — **YES** → Possible poisoning or allergic reaction. → See vet ASAP

NO

Is your dog coughing blood-tinged sputum? Does it smell of smoke? — **YES** → Possible poison or smoke inhalation. → See vet ASAP

NO

Is your dog panting intensely? Does it have a glazed expression? — **YES** → Has your dog been exposed to heat? — **YES** → Heatstroke. Cool your dog immediately. Give it water (with a little salt) to drink. → See vet ASAP

NO (from "exposed to heat?")

Has your dog recently had puppies? — **YES** → May be low calcium crisis (eclampsia). Stop puppies feeding. → See vet ASAP

NO (from panting intensely)

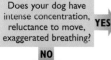

Does your dog have abnormally light breathing, twitching muscles, or cherry-red gums? — **YES** → Possible carbon monoxide poisoning. → Get fresh air to the dog. → See vet ASAP

NO

Is your dog lethargic? Does it have a fever? Is there a history of heart disease? — **YES** → See vet ASAP

NO

Does your dog have intense concentration, reluctance to move, exaggerated breathing? — **YES** → Possible fluid in chest, collapsed lung, or torn diaphragm. → See vet ASAP

NO

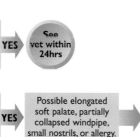

Is your dog coughing with any of: fever, listlessness, weight loss, history of heart disease? — **YES** → See vet within 24hrs

NO

Is your otherwise healthy dog snoring? — **YES** → Possible elongated soft palate, partially collapsed windpipe, small nostrils, or allergy. → See vet within 48hrs

SNORING

Dogs with flattened faces, such as Pugs, Pekingese, Boston Terriers, and Boxers have loose, slack, soft palates, and when relaxed are inclined to snore. This is also common in Cavalier King Charles Spaniels. The intensity and frequency of snoring increases with age.

If your puppy snores intensely, discuss this with your vet. Simple surgery to reduce excess soft palate tissue may be beneficial to reduce later complications.

CHANGES IN APPETITE

Dogs enjoy routine, including eating routines. A simple change of dog-food brand may be accompanied by a change of appetite. While some dogs are always hungry, an increased appetite in a dog that previously was satisfied with its portion of food may be a sign of a medical condition. A decrease in appetite almost always warrants contacting your veterinarian.

Current symptoms

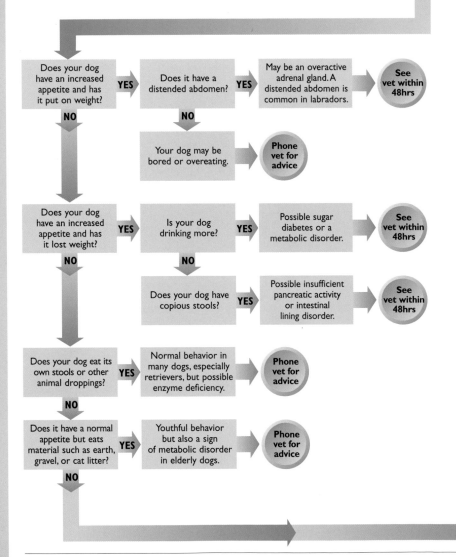

Does your dog have an increased appetite and has it put on weight? — **YES** → Does it have a distended abdomen? — **YES** → May be an overactive adrenal gland. A distended abdomen is common in labradors. → **See vet within 48hrs**

NO → Your dog may be bored or overeating. → **Phone vet for advice**

Does your dog have an increased appetite and has it lost weight? — **YES** → Is your dog drinking more? — **YES** → Possible sugar diabetes or a metabolic disorder. → **See vet within 48hrs**

NO → Does your dog have copious stools? — **YES** → Possible insufficient pancreatic activity or intestinal lining disorder. → **See vet within 48hrs**

Does your dog eat its own stools or other animal droppings? — **YES** → Normal behavior in many dogs, especially retrievers, but possible enzyme deficiency. → **Phone vet for advice**

Does it have a normal appetite but eats material such as earth, gravel, or cat litter? — **YES** → Youthful behavior but also a sign of metabolic disorder in elderly dogs. → **Phone vet for advice**

NO

COMPETITION AND THE APPETITE

There is a competitive aspect to eating. The dog has a pack instinct to fill its stomach quickly when food is available. This instinct can be triggered in even the smallest Yorkshire Terrier when it thinks there is competition for food.

HOW THE WEATHER AFFECTS EATING

Dogs often eat less in hot weather. They need more calories and eat more in cold weather. Skipping a single meal is not uncommon for many dogs, but skipping consecutive meals warrants a consultation with your veterinarian.

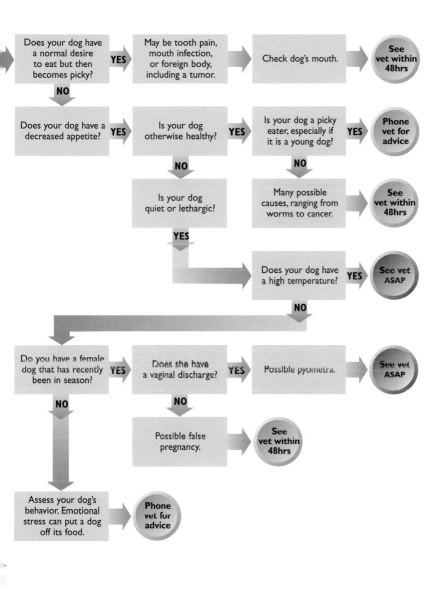

VOMITING

Lip licking, lip smacking, drooling, swallowing, and gulping are all signs of nausea and often precede vomiting. Vomiting may be caused directly by problems in the gastrointestinal system or indirectly because of conditions elsewhere in the body. Regurgitating food covered by mucous is not the same as vomiting. Regurgitating indicates a problem with the esophagus.

Current symptoms

Do you have a puppy with acute vomiting? **YES** → Possible roundworms (see page 28) and other conditions. → **See vet within 24hrs**

NO ↓

Is the vomiting projectile, black, bloody, or non-productive and continuous? **YES** → Possible obstruction, severe internal parasites, kidney or liver disease, metabolic disorder (affecting the body's chemical processes), ulcer, tumor, foreign body, bleeding disorder, or drug reaction. → **See vet ASAP**

NO ↓

Vomiting with any of: depression, fever, lethargy, weakness, restlessness, pacing, abdominal pain or distension, bloody diarrhea, dehydration, urinary difficulties, lack of balance, pale gums? **YES** → Possible bacterial or viral infection, underactive adrenal gland, twisted stomach, inflamed pancreas, bladder or inner ear problems, or severe intestinal parasites. → **See vet ASAP**

NO ↓

Is your dog regurgitating? **YES** → **See vet within 24hrs**

NO ↓

REDUCE THE RISK OF STOMACH PROBLEMS

- Do not let your dog scavenge
- Do not give bones
- Do not change your dog's diet abruptly
- Do not give toys that can be eaten or destroyed

A puppy should be routinely wormed from the age of two weeks to cure parasitic infestation.

TREATMENT FOR SIMPLE VOMITING

1 Withhold food and water.

2 Offer ice cubes or 1–3 teaspoons of soda water hourly. This will moisten your dog's mouth.

3 After 8–12 hours, offer your dog 1–3 teaspoons of regular or bland food such as chicken and rice.

4 After 8–12 hours, permit more drinking–give small amounts frequently.

5 If no further vomiting, offer more food every two hours. Return to regular diet next day.

6 If your dog is dehydrated, in shock, or has other conditions, treat it for shock (see pages 30–31). See your veterinarian immediately.

WATCH FOR SHOCK

The signs of shock are:

- Pale or white gums
- Rapid heart beat, double the normal rate
- Fast breathing, over 30 breaths per minute
- Restlessness leading to weakness

WATCH FOR DEHYDRATION

The signs of dehydration are:

- Excessive thirst
- Lethargy
- Loss of skin elasticity

If your dog has been vomiting, withhold food for 8–12 hours, then offer it a small bowl of cooked rice.

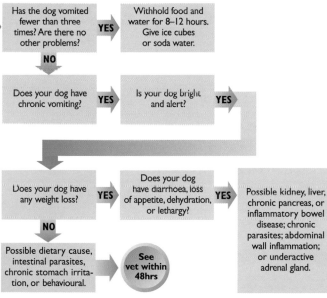

Has the dog vomited fewer than three times? Are there no other problems? **YES** → Withhold food and water for 8–12 hours. Give ice cubes or soda water.

NO

Does your dog have chronic vomiting? **YES** → Is your dog bright and alert? **YES**

Does your dog have any weight loss? **YES** → Does your dog have diarrhoea, loss of appetite, dehydration, or lethargy? **YES** → Possible kidney, liver, chronic pancreas, or inflammatory bowel disease; chronic parasites; abdominal wall inflammation; or underactive adrenal gland. → **See vet within 48hrs**

NO

Possible dietary cause, intestinal parasites, chronic stomach irritation, or behavioural. → **See vet within 48hrs**

DIARRHEA

Because dogs are opportunistic feeders, diarrhea is a common condition. Although it may be caused by parasites, infections, malabsorption problems, tumors, allergy, or metabolic disorders, diarrhea is most commonly associated with scavenging or diet changes, or what vets call dietary indiscretions. Chronic diarrhea warrants a trip to the vet.

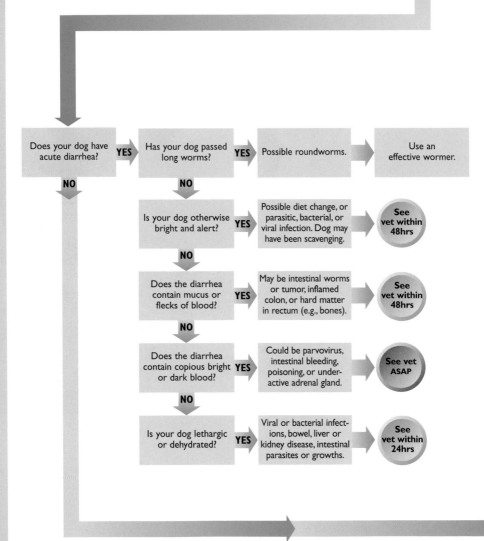

Current symptoms

Does your dog have acute diarrhea? — **YES** → Has your dog passed long worms? — **YES** → Possible roundworms. → Use an effective wormer.

NO ↓ (Does your dog have acute diarrhea?)

NO ↓ (Has your dog passed long worms?)

Is your dog otherwise bright and alert? — **YES** → Possible diet change, or parasitic, bacterial, or viral infection. Dog may have been scavenging. → See vet within 48hrs

NO ↓

Does the diarrhea contain mucus or flecks of blood? — **YES** → May be intestinal worms or tumor, inflamed colon, or hard matter in rectum (e.g., bones). → See vet within 48hrs

NO ↓

Does the diarrhea contain copious bright or dark blood? — **YES** → Could be parvovirus, intestinal bleeding, poisoning, or under-active adrenal gland. → See vet ASAP

NO ↓

Is your dog lethargic or dehydrated? — **YES** → Viral or bacterial infections, bowel, liver or kidney disease, intestinal parasites or growths. → See vet within 24hrs

DEHYDRATION

Body fluid is lost with both vomiting and diarrhea. It is also lost when a dog has a high fever, heat prostration, or no water to drink.

Dehydration can be serious. Normally, if you pinch the skin on your dog's neck, it snaps back into place immediately. Dehydration causes a loss of skin elasticity. If the skin does not retract instantly, your dog is probably dehydrated (see page 20). Contact your veterinarian immediately.

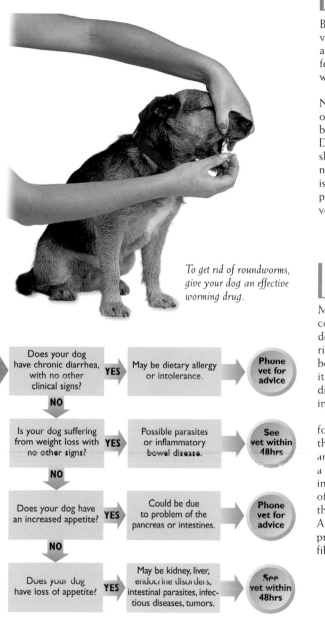

To get rid of roundworms, give your dog an effective worming drug.

HOME TREATMENT FOR DIARRHEA

Most episodes of diarrhea soon correct themselves. The affected dog quickly and efficiently gets rid of what is irritating the bowels. In these circumstances, it is best to continue feeding a diet that the "good" microbes in the intestines are used to.

Alternatively, starve your dog for 24 hours, then feed a meal that is easy to digest–chicken and rice, for example. Foods with a good balance of soluble and insoluble fiber enhance the return of "good" microbes and suppress the growth of unwanted ones. A variety of commercially produced foods is beneficial for fiber balance.

Does your dog have chronic diarrhea, with no other clinical signs? **YES**	May be dietary allergy or intolerance.	**Phone vet for advice**
NO		
Is your dog suffering from weight loss with no other signs? **YES**	Possible parasites or inflammatory bowel disease.	**See vet within 48hrs**
NO		
Does your dog have an increased appetite? **YES**	Could be due to problem of the pancreas or intestines.	**Phone vet for advice**
NO		
Does your dog have loss of appetite? **YES**	May be kidney, liver, endocrine disorders, intestinal parasites, infectious diseases, tumors.	**See vet within 48hrs**

BOWEL PROBLEMS

Mild constipation, lasting a day, is of no clinical importance and is usually caused by a dog eating something indigestible. Constipation lasting more than a day requires veterinary advice. Straining may occur with constipation, but it may also be the result of diarrhea or other reasons, and warrants professional advice or intervention.

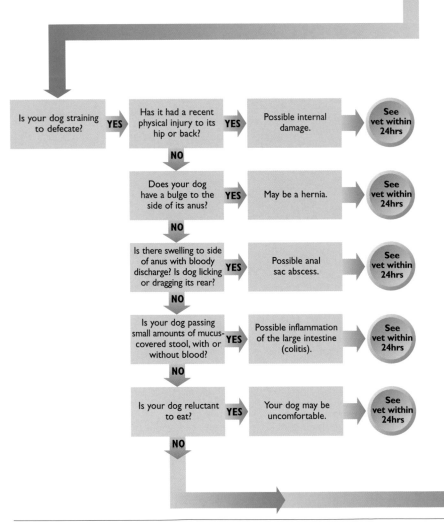

Current symptoms

Is your dog straining to defecate? **YES**

Has it had a recent physical injury to its hip or back? **YES** → Possible internal damage. → See vet within 24hrs

NO

Does your dog have a bulge to the side of its anus? **YES** → May be a hernia. → See vet within 24hrs

NO

Is there swelling to side of anus with bloody discharge? Is dog licking or dragging its rear? **YES** → Possible anal sac abscess. → See vet within 24hrs

NO

Is your dog passing small amounts of mucus-covered stool, with or without blood? **YES** → Possible inflammation of the large intestine (colitis). → See vet within 24hrs

NO

Is your dog reluctant to eat? **YES** → Your dog may be uncomfortable. → See vet within 24hrs

NO

CONSTIPATION OR DIARRHEA?

It can be easy to mistake straining associated with the inflammation of bowels already emptied by diarrhea, and straining caused by hard stools in the large intestine. Always check what has preceded an episode of straining. If your dog has just had diarrhea, it is unlikely to be straining because of constipation.

TREATING CONSTIPATION

If stools are small and hard and your dog is otherwise healthy, add fiber to the diet. Cereal bran is excellent. So, too, is canned pumpkin, which some dogs love. If your dog has not defecated for more than two days or is uncomfortable, see your vet, who may give an enema to eliminate constipation. Do not use over-the-counter enemas or laxatives made for humans. Some of these can be irritating, and even dangerous, especially to small dogs.

FEEDING BONES

The most common cause of constipation in dogs is eating indigestible substances. Bone is at the top of this list. While chewing on bone is an excellent way for a dog to massage its teeth and gums, it is also dangerous to the intestines. If you do give bones to your dog, do so only under your constant supervision. Never give your dog cooked bones. Allow your dog to benefit from some chewing and gnawing but do not let your dog swallow shards of bone. The resulting constipation is, at best, extremely painful and, at worst, actually life-threatening.

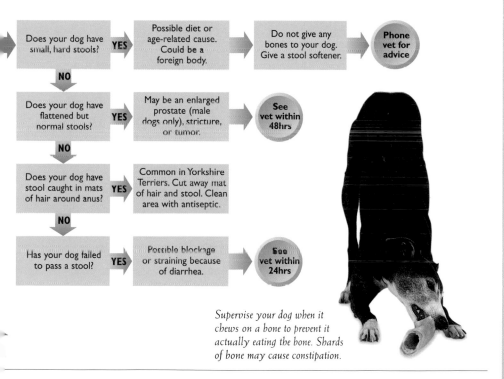

Does your dog have small, hard stools? **YES** → Possible diet or age-related cause. Could be a foreign body. → Do not give any bones to your dog. Give a stool softener. → **Phone vet for advice**

NO

Does your dog have flattened but normal stools? **YES** → May be an enlarged prostate (male dogs only), stricture, or tumor. → **See vet within 48hrs**

NO

Does your dog have stool caught in mats of hair around anus? **YES** → Common in Yorkshire Terriers. Cut away mat of hair and stool. Clean area with antiseptic.

NO

Has your dog failed to pass a stool? **YES** → Possible blockage or straining because of diarrhea. → **See vet within 24hrs**

Supervise your dog when it chews on a bone to prevent it actually eating the bone. Shards of bone may cause constipation.

EXCESSIVE DRINKING

Drinking excessively is often the first outward sign of an internal problem. It is usually, but not always, associated with excessive urinating. If your dog is drinking more than previously, this warrants a visit to your veterinarian, especially if your dog is over eight years old or from a breed prone to sugar diabetes. Whenever possible, take a urine sample to your vet.

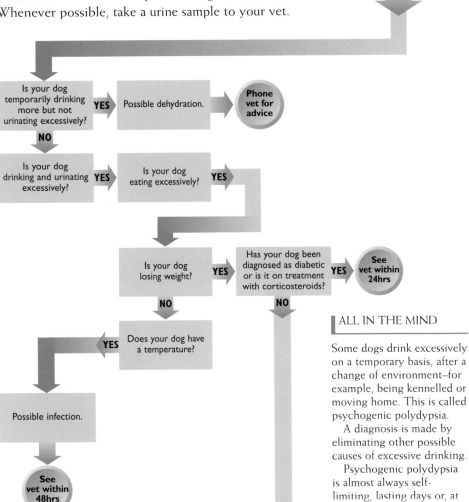

Current symptoms

Is your dog temporarily drinking more but not urinating excessively? — **YES** — Possible dehydration. → **Phone vet for advice**

NO

Is your dog drinking and urinating excessively? — **YES** — Is your dog eating excessively? — **YES**

Is your dog losing weight? — **YES** — Has your dog been diagnosed as diabetic or is it on treatment with corticosteroids? — **YES** → **See vet within 24hrs**

NO

NO

Does your dog have a temperature? — **YES**

Possible infection.

→ **See vet within 48hrs**

ALL IN THE MIND

Some dogs drink excessively on a temporary basis, after a change of environment—for example, being kennelled or moving home. This is called psychogenic polydypsia.

A diagnosis is made by eliminating other possible causes of excessive drinking.

Psychogenic polydypsia is almost always self-limiting, lasting days or, at the very most, weeks.

BREEDS AND PITUITARY DIABETES

Some breeds carry a genetic predisposition to *diabetes insipidis*, a condition in which the pituitary does not send messages to the kidneys to concentrate urine. These include the following breeds:

- Boston Terrier
- Norwegian Elkhound
- German Shepherd

Excessive drinking by your dog may be a sign of kidney or liver disease or an infection.

DRINKING AND OLDER DOGS

All dogs drink more after physical exercise, and even after mental activity. However, excessive drinking is always of clinical significance. Your older dog should not drink more than it did when it was younger. If you think your dog is drinking more, provide measured quantities for a few days, then visit your vet, bringing a morning urine sample from your dog in a clean jar, together with statistics on exactly how much it is drinking.

BREEDS AND SUGAR DIABETES

Breeds in which certain family lines have a known predisposition to diabetes include the following:

- Alaskan Malamute
- Chow Chow
- Doberman
- Finnish Spitz
- German Shepherd
- Keeshond
- Labrador
- Manchester Terrier
- Norwegian Elkhound
- Old English Sheepdog
- Poodle
- Schipperke
- Schnauzer (miniature)
- Springer Spaniel
- West Highland White Terrier
- Whippet

| Does your dog have any hair loss or a distended belly? | **YES** → | Possible overactive adrenal gland. | → | **See vet within 48hrs** |

NO ↓

| Is your dog eating normally or less than normal? | **YES** → | Does your dog have an unnatural odor, lethargy, weight loss, or vomiting? | **YES** → | Possible kidney or liver disease or failure. May be womb infection in unneutered female. | → | **See vet today** |

URINARY PROBLEMS

Urinary problems in dogs, including straining or incontinence, are not uncommon. Bacterial infection occurs for a variety of reasons, including diabetes. Bladder stones are more common in some breeds, for example Dalmatians and Dachshunds, than others. If your dog is experiencing urinary problems, always try to take a urine sample in a clean container to your vet.

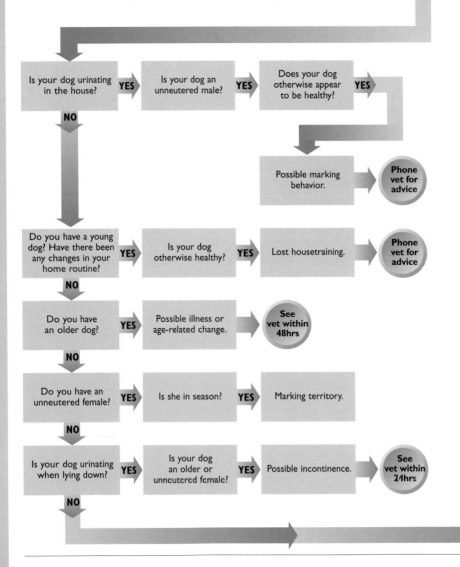

Current symptoms

Is your dog urinating in the house? **YES** Is your dog an unneutered male? **YES** Does your dog otherwise appear to be healthy? **YES**

NO

Possible marking behavior. → **Phone vet for advice**

Do you have a young dog? Have there been any changes in your home routine? **YES** Is your dog otherwise healthy? **YES** Lost housetraining. → **Phone vet for advice**

NO

Do you have an older dog? **YES** Possible illness or age-related change. → **See vet within 48hrs**

NO

Do you have an unneutered female? **YES** Is she in season? **YES** Marking territory.

NO

Is your dog urinating when lying down? **YES** Is your dog an older or unneutered female? **YES** Possible incontinence. → **See vet within 24hrs**

NO

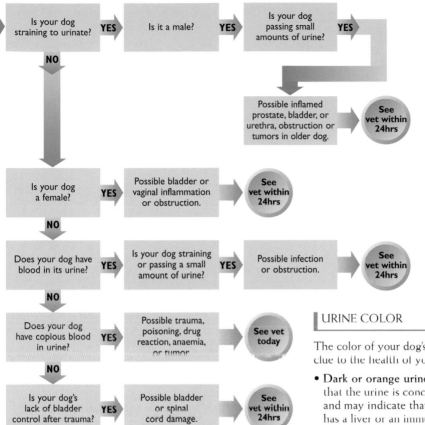

Is your dog straining to urinate? — YES → **Is it a male?** — YES → **Is your dog passing small amounts of urine?** — YES → **Possible inflamed prostate, bladder, or urethra, obstruction or tumors in older dog.** → **See vet within 24hrs**

NO ↓

Is your dog a female? — YES → **Possible bladder or vaginal inflammation or obstruction.** → **See vet within 24hrs**

NO ↓

Does your dog have blood in its urine? — YES → **Is your dog straining or passing a small amount of urine?** — YES → **Possible infection or obstruction.** → **See vet within 24hrs**

NO ↓

Does your dog have copious blood in urine? — YES → **Possible trauma, poisoning, drug reaction, anaemia, or tumor.** → **See vet today**

NO ↓

Is your dog's lack of bladder control after trauma? — YES → **Possible bladder or spinal cord damage.** → **See vet within 24hrs**

MALES AND FEMALES

The female's urinary tract is shorter and has a wider opening and diameter than that of the male. This increases her risk of bladder and urethra infections over that of the male. However, the vast majority of urinary obstructions occur in male dogs. Sediment, mucus, or bladder stones can lodge at the entrance of the urinary passage through the male's bone in the penis, causing a full obstruction. This may lead rapidly to clinical shock. Urgent veterinary attention is needed for a dog with a blocked bladder.

URINE COLOR

The color of your dog's urine is a clue to the health of your pet:

- **Dark or orange urine** means that the urine is concentrated and may indicate that your dog has a liver or an immune condition. It may also indicate dehydration or urine retention. If your dog is also lethargic, has yellow or white gums, and has lost its appetite, you should seek veterinary help immediately.

- **Light to colorless urine** means that the urine is dilute. This is usually accompanied by increased drinking (see pages 82–83) and urinating, and is often associated with *diabetes mellitus* (sugar diabetes), *diabetes insipidus* (lack of hormonal messages to concentrate), or psychogenic polydipsia (increased drinking and urinating for various behavioral reasons).

GENITAL DISCHARGES

Genital discharges are always significant. In unneutered females, a genital discharge may indicate the onset of her season or, more seriously, it may indicate mild to life-threatening infection. In male dogs, a moderate discharge from the prepuce, while messy, is normal, especially in young individuals. Excessive discharge often indicates an inflammatory problem in the sheath.

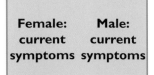

Female: current symptoms   **Male: current symptoms**

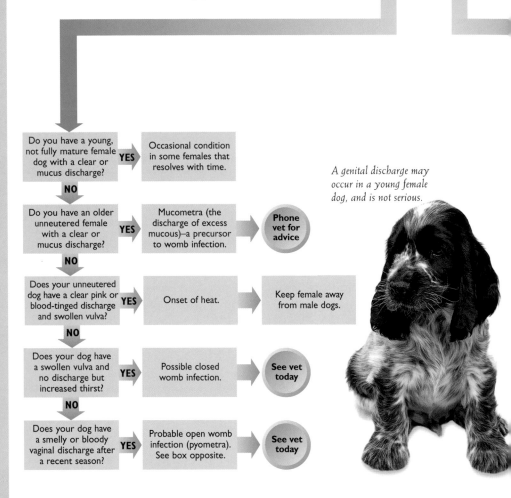

Do you have a young, not fully mature female dog with a clear or mucus discharge? **YES** → Occasional condition in some females that resolves with time.

NO

Do you have an older unneutered female with a clear or mucus discharge? **YES** → Mucometra (the discharge of excess mucous)—a precursor to womb infection. → **Phone vet for advice**

NO

Does your unneutered dog have a clear pink or blood-tinged discharge and swollen vulva? **YES** → Onset of heat. → Keep female away from male dogs.

NO

Does your dog have a swollen vulva and no discharge but increased thirst? **YES** → Possible closed womb infection. → **See vet today**

NO

Does your dog have a smelly or bloody vaginal discharge after a recent season? **YES** → Probable open womb infection (pyometra). See box opposite. → **See vet today**

A genital discharge may occur in a young female dog, and is not serious.

GENITAL OR URINARY DISCHARGE?

Irritation to the urinary system may stimulate the production of protective mucus, which is then discharged. It can be difficult to determine whether this mucus is coming from the urinary or reproductive tracts.

Your vet will examine the discharge and treat the appropriate system.

PYOMETRA

Older, unneutered females, especially those that have never produced puppies, have an ever-increasing risk of womb infection following a season. Bacteria gain access to the womb when the cervix dilates during estrous.

An individual with an open pyometra has a repellent and obvious vaginal discharge.

If the cervix closes down after infection gains entry, a closed pyometra develops. This is more toxic, more dangerous, and more difficult to diagnose. If your dog has been in season and now is off color in any way, see your vet immediately.

TIGHT PREPUCE

Young male dogs get sexually excited easily. This is seldom a problem for the dog, only an embarrassment for some owners because of the dog's timing, usually when visitors arrive. However, a small individual, such as a Yorkshire Terrier, may have a physically tight prepuce. A tight prepuce can act like an elastic band on the dog's erect penis, preventing it from retracting into its sheath. Seek veterinary advice as your dog may need help, slipping its penis back into its resting position.

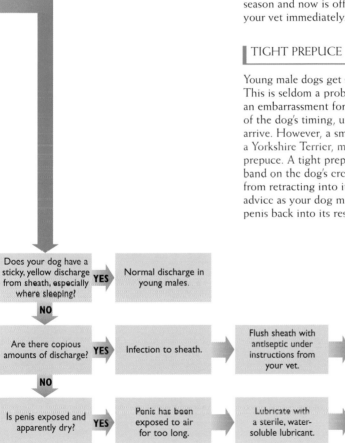

Does your dog have a sticky, yellow discharge from sheath, especially where sleeping? — **YES** → Normal discharge in young males.

NO ↓

Are there copious amounts of discharge? — **YES** → Infection to sheath. → Flush sheath with antiseptic under instructions from your vet. → **Phone vet for advice**

NO ↓

Is penis exposed and apparently dry? — **YES** → Penis has been exposed to air for too long. → Lubricate with a sterile, water-soluble lubricant. → **See vet within 24hrs**

LABOR AND BIRTH

If you know your bitch is pregnant, plan ahead. Contact your vet to ensure guidance is available when it will be needed most. Large puppies passing through a narrow birth canal may cause difficulties, as may weak contractions. Older, overweight, and nervous bitches are more likely to have weaker contractions. Maiden bitches can be late, and not know what to do.

BEFORE LABOR

A typical pregnancy is about 60–70 days. A day or so before giving birth the expectant mother eats less, gathers nesting material, and may become restless. Her body temperature drops.

Puppies are normally produced at intervals of between 30 minutes and 3 hours. Contact your vet if the interval between births is much longer.

ADVICE

Some dogs, especially small, highly strung individuals, will stop their labor if they are disturbed. To avoid this:

• Keep visitors away

• Keep all sights and sounds minimal

Current symptoms

Has your dog failed to go into labor after 66 days of pregnancy? **YES** → **Phone vet for advice**

NO

Has dog failed to go into labor 24 hours after temperature falls below 100° F (37.8° C)? **YES** → **Phone vet for advice**

NO

Has your dog failed to go into labour within one hour of first water sac being seen? **YES** → **Phone vet for advice**

NO

Has your dog failed to produce a puppy after 45 minutes of good contractions? **YES** → **Phone vet for advice**

NO

Is it more than three hours after delivery of last puppy and there seems to be more? **YES** → **Phone vet for advice**

NO

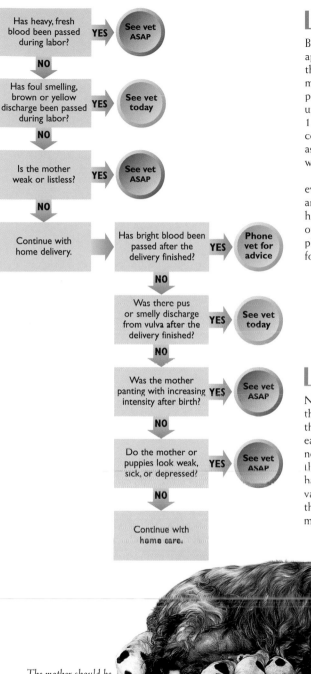

Has heavy, fresh blood been passed during labor?
YES → **See vet ASAP**
NO ↓

Has foul smelling, brown or yellow discharge been passed during labor?
YES → **See vet today**
NO ↓

Is the mother weak or listless?
YES → **See vet ASAP**
NO ↓

Continue with home delivery. → Has bright blood been passed after the delivery finished?
YES → **Phone vet for advice**
NO ↓

Was there pus or smelly discharge from vulva after the delivery finished?
YES → **See vet today**
NO ↓

Was the mother panting with increasing intensity after birth?
YES → **See vet ASAP**
NO ↓

Do the mother or puppies look weak, sick, or depressed?
YES → **See vet ASAP**
NO ↓

Continue with home care.

LABOR AND DELIVERY

Before contractions become apparent, the cervix dilates. At this time, the expectant mother may become restless, pacing and panting, lying down and getting up. This phase lasts for 4 to 12 hours, followed by visible contractions. Your dog will look as if she is trying to defecate while lying on her side.

Puppies are produced quickly, every half hour, by some mothers, and slowly, every three or more hours, by other older, weaker, or more nervous bitches. A placenta is eventually passed for each puppy.

AFTER LABOR

Natural mothers vigorously lick their newborn puppies, chew off the umbilical cords, and usually eat the placentas (which provides nourishment and hides some of the signs of birth). Typically, she has a red brown or dark green vaginal discharge, copious at first, then diminishing. This discharge may last for days or even weeks.

The mother should be alert and attentive to her newborn puppies.

GLOSSARY

Abscess A localized pocket of infection forming painful swelling.

Acute A condition that occurs suddenly, and is the opposite to chronic.

Adrenal gland Gland beside each kidney, which produces a variety of hormones, including adrenaline and cortisone.

Anaphylactic shock An exaggerated and potentially life-threatening over-reaction of the immune system. Treatment is with an injection of adrenaline.

Anemia Reduced red blood cells, caused by blood loss, bone marrow suppression, parasites, or immune-mediated disease that destroys red blood cells.

Antihistamine A drug that counteracts the effects of histamine.

Anus Outlet of the rectum.

Arthritis Inflammation of a joint.

Autoimmune disease The body's immune system erroneously attacks normal body parts.

Benign A local tumor that does not spread (that is to say, it is not malignant).

Biopsy The collection of tissue for microscopic examination.

Carcinoma A malignant tumor originating in skin cells or cells that line the internal organs.

Cardiovascular Pertaining to the heart and circulation.

Cataract Crystalline cloudiness to the lens of the eye.

Cheyletiella mites A contagious external parasite, primarily affecting young dogs and cats. Can also temporarily affect people.

Chronic Has existed for some time, as in chronic pain.

Colitis Inflammation to the large intestine, the colon.

Congenital A condition that is present at birth, and is one that may, or may not, be hereditary.

Cornea The clear surface of the eyeball. Plays important part in focusing light rays.

Cyst Liquid-filled sac that arises through disease or infection.

Dander Dry scales of skin and hair.

Degenerative necrosis A breakdown of any tissue leading to the death of that tissue.

Dehydration Loss of natural level of liquid in body tissue.

Demodex mange A non-contagious parasitic skin condition affecting mainly young or elderly dogs.

Dermatitis Inflammation to the skin.

Diabetes, insipidus Deficiency in pituitary hormone (anti-diuretic hormone, or ADH) that controls urine concentration in the kidneys. Causes excessive drinking and urinating.

Diabetes, mellitus or sugar diabetes High blood sugar, either because of a lack of insulin production or because body tissue cannot absorb circulating insulin.

Diabetic crisis A critical, life-threatening state in uncontrolled diabetes.

Diaphragm Thin involuntary muscle separating the chest cavity and abdomen.

Distemper A serious, often fatal, viral infection affecting dogs.

Dysplasia An abnormal development of tissue, usually associated with bone, as in hip dysplasia.

Ear mites Tiny parasites that live in the ear canal, causing irritation.

Eclampsia A seizure-like condition affecting nursing mothers, caused by low calcium levels in the blood.

Eczema A general term describing any type of superficial skin inflammation.

Endocrine Pertaining to the body's major hormonal systems including: the pituitary, adrenal, thyroid, and sex hormones.

Enzyme deficiency A deficiency of digestive enzymes.

Epilepsy Temporary disturbance to the nervous system caused by excessive electrical activity in the brain.

Epulis A benign tumor involving gum tissue at the margin of the teeth.

Estrous cycle The reproductive cycle.

Estrus The period in the reproductive cycle during which eggs are produced and released and the female dog is responsive to males.

Fenbendazole Wormer, with the trade-name Panacur.

Fipronil Topical flea killer, with the trade-name Frontline.

Fleas The most common external parasite living on a dog's skin and feeding on its blood.

Gastrointestinal Pertaining to the stomach and intestines.

Geriatrics An area of medicine dealing with the problems and illnesses associated with aging and the elderly.

Glaucoma Increased fluid pressure inside the eye.

Heartworms Parasites living in the heart. Larvae are transmitted by mosquitoes.

Hematoma A blood-filled swelling.

Hepatitis Inflammation of the liver.

Hereditary An inherited condition, passed on in the genes, that may occur produce symptoms at any time in life.

Hernia The protrusion of a body part out of the cavity in which it is normally located.

Hip dysplasia An abnormal development of hip joint tissue, usually leading to arthritis. Hip dysplasia is, in part, a hereditary condition.

Hookworms Blood sucking worms that live in the small intestine.

Idiopathic The cause is unknown.

Imidocloprid Topical flea killer, with the trade-name Advantage.

Immune-mediated disease A condition caused by an overreaction of the immune system.

Incontinence Uncontrolled dribble of urine, especially when dog is lying down. More common in older, neutered females.

Inflammatory bowel disease Any bowel disease associated with inflammation.

-itis An inflammation.

Kennel cough Inflammation of the throat and windpipe caused by a variety of transmissible infectious agents.

Jaundice Yellow pigmentation to the mucous membranes or skin, often due to liver disease.

Laryngitis Inflammation to the opening of the windpipe.

Laryngeal paralysis Paralysis of the voice box. Occurs primarily in large and giant breeds of dogs.

Laxative A medicine that loosens bowel contents and helps evacuation.

Leishmaniasis A protozoal disease transmitted by the bite of female sandflies.

Lice Parasites that suck blood, causing anemia in a severe infestation.

Lipoma A benign tumor of fat, especially common in older, overweight large breeds.

Litter Puppies born in a single whelping. The size of the litter varies according to the breed.

Lufenuron An insect development inhibitor used for flea control.

Lungworms Parasitic worms that invade the lungs.

Lymphoma A tumor arising from lymph tissue.

Malassezia A type of yeast that causes an itchy skin infection.

Malignant A tumor that has the potential to spread to other parts of the body.

Mastitis Inflammation of mammary (breast) tissue.

Metabolic disorder An abnormality of any of the body's metabolic functions.

Metastasize To spread to other parts of the body.

Mucometra A mucous-filled womb.

Mucus Clear, lubricating secretion produced by cells in mucous membranes.

Necrosis Cell death.

Nephritis Inflammation of the kidneys.

Neutering To castrate males or spay females to prevent reproduction and unwanted sexual behavior.

Nystagmus A ticking to the eyes caused by brain or vestibular changes.

Ophthalmologist A specialist in diseases and conditions of the eyes.

Osteochondrosis dessicans A painful condition in growing, large-breed puppies in which chips of cartilage break loose in joints.

-osis A disease condition. For example, nephrosis is a disease condition of the kidneys.

Panosteitis A self-limiting shifting lameness that occurs during growth in some medium to large breeds.

Parainfluenza One of several viruses and bacteria associated with kennel cough.

Parvovirus Virus that causes severe damage to the lining of the intestines and may also suppress the immune system.

Patella The kneecap.

Pathology The study of damaging changes to tissue.

Perianal Around the anus, as in perianal adenomas.

Perineal The regions on either side of the anus, as in perineal hernia.

Pharyngitis Inflammation of the back of the throat (pharynx).

Pleurisy Inflammation of the lining of the chest cavity.

Pneumonia Inflammation to the tissue that makes up the lungs.

Poly- Excessive or multiple, as in polyarthritis.

Polyarthritis An inflammation affecting more than one joint.

Polydypsia Excessive thirst.

Praziquantel Wormer, with the trade-name Droncit Plus.

Psychogenic Originating in the mind, as in psychogenic polydypsia.

Pulmonary Relating to the lungs.

Pus A mixture of bacteria and dead white blood cells, usually malodorous.

Pyo- Related to pus.

Pyometra A pus-filled womb.

Rabies Fatal viral disease affecting the nervous system. Usually transmitted though a bite from an infected animal.

Regurgitation Expulsion of food from the esophagus.

Retina The light-sensitive layers of cells at the back of the eyes.

Ringworm A fungal infection of the skin that causes scaly skin and mild irritation. Contrary to its name, ringworm is not caused by worms.

Roundworms Parasites that live in a dog's digestive tract, feeding on digesting food. Can cause diarrhea in puppies.

Sarcoptic mange An extremely itchy, crusty skin condition caused by *sarcoptes scabiei*, a burrowing external parasite.

Scabies Another name for the condition, sarcoptic mange.

Scent marking A dog marks its territory with urine, or with scent from special glands in its face and paws, sending a clear message to other dogs.

Sclerosis Hardening of tissue, as a consequence of age or inflammation.

Selamectin Topical flea killer, with the trade name Revolution.

Shock A medical emergency in which the cardiovascular system collapses, causing physical collapse, rapid pulse, and pale mucous membranes.

Solar dermatitis A skin inflammation triggered by exposure to intense direct sunlight. Most commonly seen in Collies.

Stricture The narrowing of a tube or passage.

Sugar diabetes See *diabetes mellitus*.

Supracaudal tail gland A vestigial territory marking gland on the dorsal surface of the tail. Sometimes becomes active or infected.

Systemic disease A disease that affects the entire body.

Tapeworms Intestinal parasites that feed on a dog's partly digested food.

Thyroid gland The gland in the neck responsible for producing hormones that control the body's metabolism.

Tonsillitis Inflammation of the tonsils.

Toxoplasmosis A contagious parasitic disease of all mammal species that rarely causes clinical signs with the exception of immune-compromised individuals. It is of concern to pregnant women.

Tumor A growth of tissue in which cell multiplication is uncontrolled and progressive.

Ulcer A lesion where surface tissue has been lost through damage or disease.

Vestibular Pertaining to the organ of balance in the middle ear, as in vestibular syndrome.

Vestibular syndrome A condition in older dogs affecting the organ of balance in the ear. Sometimes mistaken for a stroke.

Wobbler Rotation of a vertebra in the neck, most commonly seen in the large breeds such as the Great Dane. Causes a loss of balance, especially in the hind legs.

INDEX

ACKNOWLEDGMENTS

Author's acknowledgments

Produced for Dorling Kindersley Limited by Design Revolution Limited, Queens Park Villa, 30 West Drive, Brighton, East Sussex BN2 0QW

Editorial Director Ian Whitelaw
Senior Designer Lucie Penn
Project Editor Julie Whitaker

Thanks to Chris Lawrence at the RSPCA and my other veterinary colleagues for all their practical suggestions. As ever I'm grateful to my veterinary nurses, Hester Small, Hilary Hayward, Sarah Wilsdon, Amanda Hackett, Ashley McManus, and Jenny Ward for their experience and cheery efficiency running the veterinary clinic.

Publisher's acknowledgments

Dorling Kindersley would like to thank the following:

Photography
All photography by Jane Burton, Roman Clifford, Dave King, Tracy Morgan, David Ward, except:

The Kennel Club/David Dalton 10; 11; 12. Science Photo Library 29. Sally Anne Thompson Animal Photography 41.